The Free and
EQUAL.
Sweet Tooth
Cookbook

By Carole Kruppa

SURREY BOOKS
101 East Erie Street
Suite 900
Chicago, Illinois 60611

THE FREE AND EQUAL® SWEET TOOTH COOKBOOK is published by Surrey Books, 101 E. Erie Street, Suite 900, Chicago, IL 60611.

This book is manufactured in the United States of America.

ISBN: 0-940625-07-5

Library of Congress Cataloging-in-Publication Data:

Kruppa, Carole.
  Free and Equal Sweet Tooth Cookbook / by Carole Kruppa.
     p.   cm.
  Includes index.
  ISBN 0-940625-07-5
  1. Low-calorie diet—Recipes. 2. Sugar substitutes. 3. Desserts.
  I. Title.
RM222.2.K785 1988   88-22074
641.8′6—dc19   CIP

    2 3 4 5 6 7 8 9 10

Editorial production: *Bookcrafters, Inc., Chicago.*
Design and production: *Hughes & Co., Chicago.*
Illustrations: *Elizabeth Allen.*

Single copies may be ordered by sending check or money order for $9.50 (includes postage and handling) to Surrey Boks at the above address. For orders of 100 or more copies, please contact the publisher for special discounts.

This book is dedicated . . .

to my kind and supportive family and friends. First, to my husband, Harvey Stern, for patience beyond the call of duty. And to our children, Teddy, Michael, and Cherie, always willing to sample. And to my special friends who warm my heart through all of the seasons: Brian and Jenny Ackerman, Al and Dorine Anderson, Anne Carroll, Jimmy Diehl, Kim and Nancy Graff, Phil and Sheila Saperstein, David and Lillian Weiss, who always praised my efforts. And to my sister, Barbara, who is learning to love low-calorie desserts.

Acknowledgments

A book begins as a gleam in the author's eye. Before it can be a reality, many people have put many hours into producing it. This is the second book I have written for Surrey Books, and I feel that all of their people do a superior job.

I especially wish to thank my friend and publisher Susan Schwartz, whose faith in me inspires me to do my best work. My thanks also to Sally Hughes who designed this book so beautifully and to Gene DeRoin who handled the editing and production. My heart-felt appreciation goes to Joan Susic who calculated the calorie counts and the diabetic exchanges.

Equal® and NutraSweet® are registered trademarks of the NutraSweet Company. NutraSweet has neither sponsored nor is otherwise connected with this publication.

Contents

Contents

Foreword

Any initial skepticism I may have had concerning the great taste—and healthfulness—of recipes prepared with Equal® instead of sugar was laid to rest with the publication and national success of *The Free and Equal® Cookbook*. Thus, I fairly leaped at the opportunity when Carole Kruppa asked me to write the Foreword to her sequel cookbook—this time a remarkable collection of sugar-free desserts called *The Free and Equal® SWEET TOOTH Cookbook*.

"Of course," said I to Carole, "a price must be extracted for such labor, and I expect you can guess what it will be."

Knowing my weakness for desserts, Carole was quick to take my meaning.

"I know, Marty," she responded without hesitation, "you need inspiration in the form of a sample from my new cookbook. How does the Strawberry Chiffon Pie sound?"

"Wait a minute, Carole," I said, "that sounds like a lot of calories. With the help of your first book, I lost 35 pounds without sacrificing the joy of eating, and I want to keep my new wardrobe fitting. What's the bottom line on this Strawberry Chiffon creation?"

"Only 126 calories per serving, Marty."

"Send it over, Carole, and I'll see what I can come up with in the way of a Foreword."

The Strawberry Chiffon Pie arrived at my office in due course, and with some pride I announced to the staff that a special treat awaited them that morning in our coffee-break room. By mid-morning I finally had a few moments to spare and hurried toward the treat I had been anticipating. To my astonishment, only one slim piece remained. I devoured it with gusto.

How can something as good as that Strawberry Chiffon Pie have so few calories, I asked myself? The answer came quickly. Carole's pies, cakes, cookies, and sweets simply contain no added sugar. Instead of the 32 calories you get with two teaspoons of sugar, the equivalent packet of Equal® contains only 4. And Equal®'s clean flavor without after-taste makes it an ideal sugar substitute.

But the healthfulness of the recipes in this book goes well beyond the benefits of just reducing calorie intake. These desserts, drinks, and confections are also carefully controlled to reduce fat, lower cholesterol, and minimize sodium. Even diabetic exchanges have been taken into account for those on special diets. No butter is used, vegetable spray replaces oil, and skim milk replaces whole.

Good news to a sweets-loving cardiologist such as myself! To her everlasting credit, Carole Kruppa has figured out a way to solve the dessert-lover's dilemma: how to have your sweets and control your diet, too.

That evening, with the memory of the Strawberry Chiffon Pie still fresh in my mind, I sat down to fulfill my part of the bargain. What a pleasure it will be, I thought, to tell people about the great-tasting—and eminently healthful—recipes they will find in *The Free and Equal® SWEET TOOTH Cookbook*.

I. Martin Grais, M.D.
Clinical Cardiology Group, Ltd.
Chicago, Illinois

Introduction

Welcome to *The Free and Equal® Sweet Tooth Cookbook*, a collection of delicious, reduced-calorie dessert and beverage recipes made with Equal®, the low-calorie sweetener. Eating light, a trend that began about five years ago, is now a way of life for many of us. This book is the result of listening to family and friends who found it necessary to lose weight or to reduce their intake of cholesterol, fat, and sodium.

Although many dieters may be willing to cut out big meals and eat smaller portions, few are willing to eliminate desserts forever. Too many diets allow only fresh fruit or a small slice of angel food cake for dessert. Few people can be satisfied by that for very long. In addition, those dieters who cook for a family will be happy to know that at last there are some great-tasting, low-calorie sweets the entire family can enjoy.

Are you a diabetic who has to avoid sugar? Do you have hypoglycemia (low blood sugar)? Has your doctor suggested that you lower your cholesterol, fat, or sodium consumption? If so, *The Free and Equal® Sweet Tooth Cookbook* is for you!

My hope is that you purchased this book because you have made a commitment to improve your eating habits and provide better family nutrition. *The Free and Equal® Sweet Tooth Cookbook* will help you meet both these objectives in a delicious and healthy way.

Before trying any of these luscious treats, be sure to read the following tips about preparing recipes with

1

Equal®. Also look for the helpful hints before each chapter to insure the best possible results.

Note: Equal® (aspartame) should not be used by people suffering from the hereditary disease known as phenylketonuria (PKU). These people must restrict their intake of protein foods containing phenylalanine, one of the amino acids in aspartame. Fortunately, phenylketonuria is a rare disease.

Why This Cookbook Is Unique

- These recipes are special.
- No recipe calls for sugar.
- Most of the desserts are below 200 calories per serving; some are even lower than 100 calories!
- The recipes are low in cholesterol, saturated fats, and sodium.
- The American Heart Association* guidelines for a healthy diet have guided me in developing these recipes. The AHA diet can help you: 1) Meet your daily needs for protein, vitamins, minerals, and other nutrients; 2) Reach and maintain your most desirable weight; 3) Lower your fat intake to about 30 percent of the calories you consume; 4) Limit foods containing saturated fat and cholesterol.

Additional guidelines to consider include the following:

1. *Variety Without Excess*
This is the first essential diet rule. If we eat a variety of basic foods—vegetables and fruits; whole grain and en-

---

*The American Heart Association provides free information and diets in a publication called "Heartline." To receive it, send a stamped, self-addressed envelope with your request to your local AHA chapter.

riched cereals and breads; poultry, fish, and meat; dairy products; eggs; fats and oils—we will receive most of the nutrients we need. It is the nutrients (carbohydrates, proteins, fats, vitamins, and minerals in addition to fiber and water) that are essential, not specific foods themselves.

2. *Maintain Ideal Weight*

Obesity has been called the number one public health problem in the country. Approximately 40 percent of all Americans are overweight (at least 10 percent above ideal body weight). Maintaining your ideal body weight is a key part of staying healthy. If you are among the lucky, already at your ideal weight, or are like most of us, struggling to get there, these recipes can help you. Everyone looks forward to dessert at the end of their meal, but most of us are concerned about the excessive calories often found in them.

3. *Avoid Too Much Fat, Cholesterol, and Sodium.*

Fat remains a problem in the American diet. With the increase of fast-food outlets, labor saving devices, and a dependence on the automobile, Americans have markedly decreased physical activity levels compared with earlier periods. The American diet has evolved from natural foods with complex carbohydrates and minimal fat content to a high-fat, highly-refined carbohydrate diet of prepared foods. With these dietary changes has come an increased incidence of obesity and the associated problems of diabetes mellitus, hypertension, atherosclerotic cardiovascular disease, and hyperlipidemia. Diets high in sodium have been linked to health problems such as high blood pressure. The major source of sodium is salt (sodium chloride). Many Americans eat five times as much salt as they need. One of the easiest ways to minimize the amount of salt you eat may be to cut down or eliminate adding salt at the table and in cooking. Instead, enhance natural flavors by minimal cooking and a few carefully selected herbs and spices.

4. *Eat Foods with Adequate Starch and Fiber*

Foods that are high in starch and fiber generally contain a wide variety of essential vitamins and minerals. They also are important because they add bulk to your diet. Hence, they fill you up, often for very few calories. Fruits are excellent sources of fiber, and they appear frequently in these recipes. Consider the fact that you probably could not eat more than two apples at a sitting, yet it might take six or seven chocolate chip cookies (65 calories each and very little fiber) to make you feel equally full. Surprise! the two apples contain only 160 calories.

5. *Avoid Too Much Sugar*

Sugar, like starch, is a source of carbohydrate; however, foods that contain sugar as a major ingredient generally have few vitamins and minerals. You could probably lose ten pounds effortlessly in one year just by eliminating two tablespoons of sugar a day from your diet. The desserts in this book will save you hundreds of calories per serving. Just think of what that can do for your figure!

6. *Use Alcohol Moderately*

If you drink alcoholic beverages, do so in moderation. Or skip them altogether, substituting for them one of the spirits-enhanced desserts in this book.

How To Use This Book

In order to make it easier for you to use these recipes, we are including the following information:

Calories: The calories contained in each serving are listed. While these recipes are much lower than traditional recipes, remember that moderation is the key, and keep your servings within our guidelines.

Food Exchange: Our food exchanges have been prepared according to the food exchanges developed by the American Diabetes and Dietetic Associations, and the exchanges per serving of each recipe are listed.

Heart Symbol: ♥ : A heart symbol designates recipes that are particularly low in cholesterol, saturated fats, and sodium.

Microwave: The majority of these recipes use conventional cooking methods, but some can be adapted easily to the microwave. All of these are clearly marked. A few of the desserts require cooking in a microwave and are so noted.

Tips: At the beginning of each chapter, a list of "Tips" has been included to pass along some hints on how to make these recipes more successful. To insure best results, please read the "Tips" before preparing the dessert.

Brand Index: To help you find some of the products we used in the recipes, I have listed those that I felt produced the best results. But feel free to experiment on your own.

Garnishes: Suggestions for ways to garnish each dessert are provided because I believe they will be as pleasing to the eye as to the palate. Garnishes are optional and have not been calculated in the exchanges given per serving.

PREPARING RECIPES WITH EQUAL®

- Equal® should be added to recipes *after* cooking; prolonged exposure to oven or range heat will reduce the sweetness.
- Equal® does not provide the volume or structure of sugar; thus Equal® is not recommended for all cooking and baking.
- These desserts tend to be lighter in texture than traditional desserts because alternative ingredients such as ricotta and cottage cheese, non-fat yogurt, and skim milk are used. This also keeps calories and fat to a minimum.
- The degree of sweetness in a recipe will depend on your own sweet tooth; you will find that some recipes will require more, some less Equal®, depending on your taste buds.
- The recipes in this book have been developed for use with Equal®. Success is not assured if another sweetener or method of preparation is used.

What Is Equal®?

Equal® contains a sweetening ingredient called aspartame. Aspartame is a dipeptide composed of two naturally-occurring amino acids. This is why it can be said that Equal® is made from constituents of protein that occur naturally in many foods. Like sugar, it is nutritive in that it is used by the body like food.

Unlike other low-calorie sweeteners, Equal® has a clean, sweet taste, with no unpleasant after-taste. Equal® does not contain saccharin or sodium.

Cookies and Snacks

The cooky jar brings back memories that most of us cherish. Crisp, crunchy drop cookies, chewy bar cookies, or pretty rolled and pressed cookies; we remember them all. They can be plain or fancy, made ahead, or quickly baked at a moment's notice. They're right for any occasion, whether it's a picnic or a dinner party. They also make excellent gifts for friends or family.

The recipes in this chapter will satisfy the cookie monster in you, and they are designed to help you keep low-calorie, ready to eat goodies on hand. This will reduce your urge to splurge on high-calorie alternatives. See if you don't agree that they're the very best of the batch.

Tips for Successful Cookies and Snacks

- Make decorative cookies fast. Prepare batches of cookie doughs, pat each into a rectangle, stack, chill well, and slice.
- Juice cans make good molds for cookies. Pack dough in the can and chill. At baking time, remove the bottom of the can. (Use a can opener that cuts a smooth edge.) Press against the bottom to push out dough—just enough to make a $\frac{1}{8}$-to-$\frac{1}{4}$-inch-thick cooky. Cut with a sharp knife, and place dough on an ungreased cooky sheet. Repeat procedure until all dough is used.
- Ball cookies will be even in size if you pat the dough into a long roll first. Then divide it: first in half, then in quarters, then in eighths, depending on what size cooky you want.
- Using only one batch of dough, you can make a plateful of different looking cookies. After shaping the dough, leave some plain; press others with a fork to produce a crisscross pattern. With a spoon, make a hollow in some to fill with jam after baking; or top some with a cherry or walnut half.
- Wrap cookies individually or in back-to-back pairs. If you are planning to give cookies as a gift, line a gift box or tin with cellophane or waxed paper, and place a cushion of crumpled paper on the bottom. Layer the cookies alternately with cushioning material, leaving space for a final layer of cushioning on top.
- If you are making your own graham cracker crumbs, use 12 two-inch squares for 1 cup of crushed crumbs. A food processor or blender works wonders for crushing crackers, wafers, or zwieback. You can also crush with a rolling pin: break up the crackers, put them in a plastic bag, and roll.

Tropical Popcorn

3 tablespoons diet margarine, melted
½ teaspoon ground cinnamon
8 cups popped corn (popped without
    salt or fat)
1 cup chopped, dried mixed fruit
3½ ounces banana chips
2 packets Equal®

Combine margarine and cinnamon; stir well. Drizzle over popped corn, tossing gently to coat. Add chopped dried fruit, bananas, and Equal®. Store in an airtight container.

Makes 8 (1-cup) servings.
Calories per serving: 150.
Diabetic exchanges per serving: milk 0,
    vegetable 0, fruit 1, bread 1, meat 0, fat 0.

Orange Yogurt Pops

2 cups plain yogurt
1 can (6 oz.) frozen orange juice
    concentrate
1 teaspoon vanilla
8 packets Equal®
Popsicle sticks

Combine all ingredients in a blender. Pour into 8, 3-oz. paper cups. Insert a Popsicle stick in the center of each. Freeze until firm. Unmold by briefly dipping each cup in hot water.

Makes 8 pops.
Calories per pop: 74.
Diabetic exchanges per pop: milk 0,
    vegetable 0, fruit 1, bread 0, meat 0, fat 0.

Date Bars

¾ cup chopped dates
2 tablespoons diet margarine
1 egg
1 tablespoon skim milk
1 teaspoon vanilla extract
4 packets Equal®
3 cups toasted rice cereal
¼ cup unsweetened coconut, chopped

Mix chopped dates, margarine, egg, milk, and vanilla in a medium saucepan. Place over medium heat about 5 minutes until mixture is thick. Cool, then stir in Equal® and cereal. For bars, press mixture into an 8-inch square pan, sprayed with vegetable spray. Sprinkle with coconut and refrigerate until firm. Cut into 24 bars.

Makes 12 servings of 2 bars each.
Calories per servings: 83.
Diabetic exchanges per serving: milk 0,
    vegetable 0, fruit 0, bread 1, meat 0, fat 0.

Lemon Drops ♥

36 vanilla cookies (Estee dietetic)
3 tablespoons lemon juice
¼ teaspoon lemon extract
4 packets Equal®

Crush cookies until very fine. Mix the cookie crumbs with the lemon juice, lemon extract, and Equal®. Divide mixture into 2 parts. Divide each part into 14 pieces. Roll each piece into a ball.

Lemon drops are a nice treat for a tea, shower, or card party.

Makes 14 servings of 2 cookies each.
Calories per serving: 54.
Diabetic exchanges per serving: milk 0,
    vegetable 0, fruit 1, bread 0, meat 0, fat 0.

Heavenly Fudge ♥

½ cup canned crushed pineapple, no
    sugar added
⅓ cup nonfat dry milk powder
2 teaspoons unsweetened cocoa
2 packets Equal®

In medium bowl, combine all ingredients until no
traces of milk powder or cocoa remain. Turn mixture
into an individual loaf pan or a 10-oz. custard cup and
place in freezer until firm.

Makes 1 serving.
Calories per serving: 135.
Diabetic exchanges per serving: milk 1,
    vegetable 0, fruit 1, bread 0, meat 0, fat 0.

Almond Crescents

¼ cup plus 1 tablespoon diet marga-
    rine, room temperature
1½ tablespoons light honey
¼ cup ground, blanched almonds
1 cup sifted whole-wheat pastry flour
1 teaspoon almond extract
9 packets Equal®
1 teaspoon cinnamon

Preheat oven to 300°. Beat margarine in large bowl of
electric mixer until light and creamy. Add honey and
mix well. Add almonds and beat again. Stir in flour
and almond extract with wooden spoon. Lightly flour a
baking sheet.
    Roll small handful of dough between palms to form
short cylinder. Transfer to work surface, and use palm
to roll into longer cylinder about ⅜-inch thick. Cut into
2 separate pieces. Transfer to prepared baking sheet.
Bend ends of pieces to form crescents, or half-moons.
Repeat with remaining dough. Bake 20 to 25 minutes.
Cool on wire rack.

Put Equal® and cinnamon in a small bowl. Mix well. Dredge each cookie in the Equal®-cinnamon mixture and set aside. Store in container. *Makes about 3 dozen cookies.*

> *Makes 12 servings of 3 cookies each.*
> *Calories per serving: 82.*
> *Diabetic exchanges per serving: milk 0,*
> *vegetable 0, fruit 0, bread 1, meat 0, fat 0.*

Cream cheese pastry.

Cream Cheese Pinwheels

> 1 cup diet margarine* at room
>   temperature
> 1 package (8 oz.) cream cheese at
>   room temperature
> 2 cups all-purpose flour
> ¼ cup fruit-only apricot preserves
> ¼ cup fruit-only strawberry preserves
> ¼ cup pecans chopped fine
> 5 packets Equal®

Beat margarine and cream cheese in a large bowl with electric mixer until well blended and smooth. With electric mixer on low speed, add flour; beat until blended. Divide dough into fourths. Shape each into a rectangle and flatten to 1-inch thickness. Wrap and refrigerate overnight or until firm enough to roll.

Heat oven to 350°. Have cookie sheets ready. Work with one portion of dough at a time. On a lightly-floured surface with floured rolling pin, roll dough out to a 10 × 7½-inch rectangle; trim edges. With sharp knife, cut into 2½-inch squares. Place squares 1 inch apart on ungreased cookie sheets.

For pinwheels, drop ½ teaspoon of preserves in the center of each square. Starting from tips, slit corner of each square 1 inch toward center. Fold every other half-corner to center like a pinwheel, overlapping the tips. Pinch firmly in center. Sprinkle center with nuts.

Bake 13 to 15 minutes until tips are lightly browned. Remove from oven and place on racks to cool. While cookies are still warm, place Equal® in a flour sifter and sift Equal® over cookies.

Makes 16 servings of 3 pinwheels each.
Calories per serving: 195.
Diabetic exchanges per serving: milk 0,
    vegetable 0, fruit 1½, bread 0, meat 0, fat 2.

*NOTE: Do not use margarine with liquid oil listed as the first ingredient.

Old-Fashioned Thumbprint Cookies

½ cup diet margarine, softened
1 egg
½ teaspoon vanilla
1¼ cups flour
½ cup finely chopped nuts
3 packets Equal®
Strawberry or raspberry fruit-only jam

Beat together shortening, egg, vanilla, and enough flour so dough is no longer sticky. Work in nuts. Chill until firm enough to shape (about 30 minutes). Roll into balls. Place on ungreased cookie sheet. Dip your thumb in flour. Press down firmly in the middle of each cookie. Bake 15 minutes or until golden brown on the bottoms. Remove from oven. Sprinkle with Equal®. Cool. Fill hollows with jam. Keep refrigerated.

Makes 5 servings of 3 cookies each.
Calories per serving: 98.
Diabetic exchanges per serving: milk 0,
    vegetable 0, fruit 0, bread ½, meat 0, fat 1.

Peanut Butter Bites

½ cup skimmed milk
½ cup diet margarine
½ cup creamy peanut butter
1 cup raisins
1 teaspoon vanilla
10 packets Equal®
3 cups quick-cooking oats

In a heavy saucepan, bring milk, shortening, and peanut butter to a boil. Remove from heat. Add raisins, vanilla, and Equal®. Mix well. Work in oats, a cup at a time. Form into small balls about 1½ in. diameter. Place on a cookie sheet. Chill. Keep refrigerated and covered.

Makes 12 servings of 2 cookies each.
Calories per serving: 214.
Diabetic exchanges per serving: milk 0,
    vegetable 0, fruit 0, bread 2, meat 0, fat 2.

Crunchy Grape-Nuts Cookies

½ cup diet margarine
⅓ cup skimmed milk
½ teaspoon cinnamon
1 cup quick-cooking oats
1 cup Post Grape-Nuts
10 packets Equal®
1 cup chopped walnuts

In a heavy saucepan, bring shortening and milk to a boil. Remove from heat. Stir in remaining ingredients. Mix well. Form into 1-inch balls. Place on cookie sheet. Chill until firm. Keep refrigerated.

Makes 6 servings of 4 cookies each.
Calories per serving: 162.
Diabetic exchanges per serving: milk 0,
    vegetable 0, fruit 0, bread 1, meat 0, fat 2.

Choco Ball Cookies

> ¼ cup unsweetened cocoa
> ½ cup skimmed milk
> ½ cup diet margarine
> 3 cups quick-cooking oats
> 2 teaspoons vanilla
> ½ cup unsweetened, shredded
>   coconut
> 10 packets Equal®

Bring cocoa, milk, and shortening to a boil. Cook for 1 minute, stirring constantly. Remove from heat. Stir in remaining ingredients. Form into balls and place on a cookie sheet. Chill until firm. Keep refrigerated.

> *Makes 12 servings of 2 cookies each.*
> *Calories per serving: 140.*
> *Diabetic exchanges per serving: milk 0,*
>   *vegetable 0, fruit 0, bread 1, meat 0, fat 1.*

Apricot and Date Bars

> 2 cups chopped apricots (dried)
> 2 cups chopped dates
> 1 cup unsweetened, crushed
>   pineapple
> ¾ cup water
> 1 tablespoon vanilla
> 2 cups whole-wheat flour
> ⅔ cup oat flakes (may be chopped in
>   blender)
> 1 cup diet margarine
> ½ cup unsweetened coconut
>   (optional)
> ½ cup finely chopped nuts (optional)
> 4 packets Equal®

Combine apricots, dates, pineapple, water and cook until thick and smooth. Add vanilla. Set fruit mixture aside. Combine remaining ingredients to form a crumb mixture. Pour one half of the mixture into greased 9 × 12-in. pan. Firmly press to make a crust. Add fruit mixture, then remaining topping. Pat down well. Bake at 350° for 30 minutes or until light brown. Let cool and then sprinkle with 4 packets of Equal®. Cut into squares.

Makes 12 servings of 2 bars each.
Calories per serving: 127.
Diabetic exchanges per serving: milk 0,
*   vegetable 0, fruit 1, bread ½, meat 0, fat 1.*

Orange Drops ♥

    36 vanilla cookies (Estee dietetic)
    2 tablespoons orange juice concentrate
    3 packets Equal®
    3 tablespoons unsweetened coconut,
        finely chopped.

Crush cookies until fine. Mix cookie crumbs with orange juice concentrate, Equal®, and coconut. Divide mixture into 2 parts. Divide each part into 10 pieces. Roll each piece into a ball.

Makes 5 servings of 4 cookies each.
Calories per serving: 96.
Diabetic exchanges per serving: milk 0, vegeta-
*   ble 0, fruit 1½, bread 0, meat 0, fat 0.*

Chocolate Coconut Bonbons ♥

    4 zwieback rounds
    1 teaspoon cocoa powder
    2 tablespoons water
    4 packets Equal®
    1 tablespoon unsweetened coconut,
        finely chopped

Crush zwieback until very fine. Mix cocoa and water, then add zwieback and remaining ingredients. Divide mixture into 2 parts. Divide each part into 10 pieces (approximately ½ teaspoon each). Roll each piece into a ball.

Serve these chewy, chocolate cookies with a hot cup of cocoa.

> *Makes 20 bonbons.*
> *Calories, each: 18.*
> *Diabetic exchanges, each: milk 0, vegetable 0,*
>   *fruit 0, bread 0, meat 0, fat 0.*

Peanut Butter Balls ♥

36 vanilla cookies (Estee dietetic)
2 tablespoons peanut butter
2 tablespoons skim milk
2 tablespoons peanuts, finely chopped
4 packets Equal®

Crush cookies until very fine. Mix the peanut butter with the skim milk. Add the cookie crumbs, Equal®, and chopped peanuts. Divide mixture into 4 parts. Divide each part into 7 pieces. Roll each piece into a ball.

> *Makes 14 servings of 2 cookies each.*
> *Calories per serving: 47.*
> *Diabetic exchanges per serving: milk 0,*
>   *vegetable 0, fruit 0, bread ½, meat 0, fat 0.*

Desserts To Sip

There's nothing under the summer sun more refreshing than a drink—ideally, a tall, cool beverage you sip slowly while watching a boat sail by or sea gulls glide across the sea. As a child, one of my favorite pastimes was to sit under the big apple tree watching the world go by as I sipped an egg cream.

Now that I live in the Midwest, where winters can be very cold, I have learned the pleasures of warm drinks enjoyed by a blazing fire. Whether it's 100° in the shade or 30 below, a dessert you sip can be very satisfying. You will also find a number of drinks to serve with desserts that complement them and give guests the option of choosing which they prefer.

Tips for Successful Dessert Drinks

- Cold drinks are more appealing if served in frosted glasses. Place the glasses in the freezer at least 30 minutes before serving.
- Coffee and teas will stay fresh if you store them in your freezer. Be sure to store them in tightly-sealed containers. This tip is provided for those of you that don't drink coffee or tea on a daily basis.
- When you make punch, decorate the punch bowl with a fruited ice ring. To do this, take a metal or plastic ring mold and fill it with water. Add small bunches of grapes, orange and lemon slices, strawberries, or mint leaves. Freeze the mold and unmold the ring at serving time by running it quickly under hot water. Place the ring in the punch bowl. You can also put small fruits into ice cubes for a festive touch.
- Use fruits as edible stirrers and garnishes. Pineapple chunks, orange, lemon and lime slices, or strawberries are excellent garnishes. I like to purchase wooden kabobs at party shops to use as decorative stirrers. Just pile several fruits on each and place in the glass. This provides a stirrer as well as a garnish. Pineapple can be cut into long strips to use as stirrers as well. You can add red and green cherries to the kabobs for variety. For warm, winter drinks I like to add a cinnamon stick as a stirrer and a garnish.
- You can also make fruit-flavored ice cubes that become part of the drink. Just fill an ice cube tray with fruit juice and freeze.
- Cloves can be a nice addition to your drink if you want a spicy pick-up.

The addition of strawberries gives this drink a rosy pink glow.

Strawberry Kiss ♥

5 to 6 strawberries
½ cup crushed ice
1 cup sparkling mineral water or club
    soda*
1 packet Equal®
1 whole strawberry for garnish

*White wine can be substituted for the mineral water.

Hull and cut up strawberries and place in a blender container. Add ice, mineral water, and Equal®. Cover and blend on high speed until mixture is smooth. Pour into a large glass. Garnish with whole strawberry.

Makes 1 serving.
Calories per serving (with mineral water): 50.
Diabetic exchanges per serving (with mineral water):
    milk 0, vegetable 0, fruit 1, bread 0, meat 0, fat 0.

Calories per serving (with wine): 200.
Diabetic exchanges per serving (with wine): milk 0,
    vegetable 0, fruit 1, bread 0, meat 0, fat 3.

Cantaloupe Smoothee

½ ripe cantaloupe
¾ cup skim milk
1 cup low-fat yogurt (plain)
¾ cup crushed ice
1 packet Equal®

Peel the cantaloupe and remove the seeds. Cut into 1-inch cubes, and put into the bowl of a blender. Add milk, yogurt, crushed ice, and Equal®, and blend at highest speed until thick and smooth.

Other fruit such as strawberries, raspberries, or bananas can be used.

Makes 2 servings.
Calories per serving: 135.
Diabetic exchanges per serving: milk 1½,
vegetable 0, fruit 0, bread 0, meat 0, fat 0.

Buttermilk-Fruit Coolers

3 cups buttermilk
2 packets Equal®
1 teaspoon vanilla
1 cup frozen, unsweetened sliced
     peaches, strawberries, or
     blueberries

In blender container, combine buttermilk, Equal®, and vanilla. Add desired frozen fruit; cover and blend 30 seconds or till smooth. Pour into glasses; garnish with fresh fruit if desired.

Makes 6 (5-ounce) servings.
Calories per serving: 63.
Diabetic exchanges per serving: milk ½,
vegetable 0, fruit ½, bread 0, meat 0, fat 0.

South of the Border Hot Chocolate ♥

⅓ cup water
3 tablespoons unsweetened cocoa
     powder
3½ inches of stick cinnamon
3 cups skim milk
¼ teaspoon vanilla
2 packets Equal®

In saucepan, combine water, unsweetened cocoa powder, and stick cinnamon. Bring to a boil, stirring constantly; boil 1 minute longer. Stir in the skim milk. Cook till heated through (do not boil). Add vanilla. Remove the stick cinnamon. Stir in the Equal®. Beat with a rotary beater. Garnish each serving with a cinnamon stick.

> *Makes 4 (6-ounce) servings.*
> *Calories per serving: 170.*
> *Diabetic exchanges per serving: milk 1,*
>   *vegetable 0, fruit 0, bread 0, meat 0, fat 0.*

Pink Lemonade

5 cups water
1 cup lemon juice
10 packets Equal®
3 tablespoons grenadine syrup
Lemon slices (optional)
Mint sprigs (optional)

Combine all ingredients. Serve over ice. Garnish with mint sprigs or lemon slices.

> *Makes 6 (1-cup) servings.*
> *Calories per serving: 40.*
> *Diabetic exchanges per serving: milk 0,*
>   *vegetable 0, fruit ½, bread 0, meat 0, fat 0.*

Adam's Tea ♥

7 cups water
10 dried apple slices
1 teaspoon ground cardamom
1 teaspoon ground cinnamon
4 cinnamon-apple herb tea bags
3 Irish breakfast or other black tea bags
7 packets of Equal®

Combine first 4 ingredients in large saucepan; bring to a boil. Reduce heat and simmer 15 minutes. Remove from heat. Add tea bags, cover, and let stand 10 minutes. Discard tea bags. Add Equal® and let stand to cool. Serve over ice cubes, and top each glass with an apple slice.

Makes 5 (1-cup) servings.
Calories per serving: 15.
Diabetic exchanges per serving: milk 0,
    vegetable 0, fruit 0, bread 0, meat 0, fat 0.

Thick, Fruity Milk Shakes ♥

    1 cup skim milk
    2 medium bananas, peeled, cut up,
        and frozen
    1 cup chopped fresh or frozen
        peaches or strawberries; or 1 cup
        fresh or frozen blueberries
    ½ cup low-fat, cream-style cottage
        cheese
    1 packet Equal®
    5 large ice cubes

In a blender container or food processor bowl, combine milk, fruits, cottage cheese, and Equal®. Cover and blend, gradually adding ice till smooth.

Makes 4 servings.
Calories per serving: 116.
Diabetic exchanges per serving: milk 0,
    vegetable 0, fruit 1½, bread 0, meat ½, fat 0.

Grasshopper Shake ♥

    1 cup mint sherbet (page 124)
    1 cup skim milk
    Mint leaves (optional)

Blend sherbet and milk together in blender until shake is smooth and thick. Serve immediately. Garnish with a fresh mint leaf.

Makes 2 servings.
Calories per serving: 100.
Diabetic exchanges per serving: milk 1,
    vegetable 0, fruit 0, bread 0, meat 0, fat 0.

Banana Shake ♥

1 banana, peeled and sliced
2 packets Equal®
2 cups skim milk
Dash cinnamon

Put banana, Equal®, and milk in a blender and blend on high setting until banana is liquefied. Pour mixture into tall glasses and top with a dash of cinnamon.

Makes 2 servings.
Calories per serving: 145.
Diabetic exchanges per serving: milk 1,
    vegetable 0, fruit 1, bread 0, meat 0, fat 0.

Café au Lait ♥

2 cups skim milk
2 cups water
1½ tablespoons instant coffee
2 packets Equal®
4 tablespoons non-dairy whipped
    topping
Dash nutmeg

Heat milk and water in a medium saucepan but do not boil. Stir in coffee and Equal® until both dissolve. Pour into 4 cups. Garnish with whipped topping and a dash of nutmeg.

Makes 4 (1-cup) servings.
Calories per serving: 55.
Diabetic exchanges per serving: milk ½,
*   vegetable 0, fruit 0, bread 0, meat 0, fat 0.*

Mock Orange Julius ♥

½ of 6-oz. can of frozen orange juice
**   concentrate, undiluted**
½ cup each: skim milk and water
½ teaspoon vanilla
2 packets Equal®
6 to 8 medium ice cubes

Combine orange juice concentrate, milk, water,
vanilla, and Equal® in blender container. Blend at high
speed. Add ice cubes and blend till cubes are dissolved.

Makes 4 servings.
Calories per serving: 48.
Diabetic exchanges per serving: milk 0,
*   vegetable 0, fruit 1, bread 0, meat 0, fat 0.*

Peach Frostee ♥

1 can (16 oz.) peach slices in juice
½ cup dry milk powder
1 teaspoon vanilla
Dash of cinnamon
5 ice cubes

In a blender container, combine canned sliced
peaches, dry milk powder, vanilla, and cinnamon.
Cover and blend till smooth. Add 5 ice cubes, one at a
time with the motor running. Blend till smooth.

Makes 2 servings.
Calories per serving: 115.
Diabetic exchanges per serving: milk 1,
*   vegetable 0, fruit ½, bread 0, meat 0, fat 0.*

Pineapple Punch

1½ cups cold water
6 inches of stick cinnamon
12 whole cloves
6 packets Equal®
1 can (46 oz.) unsweetened pineapple
    juice
1½ cups orange juice
½ cup lemon juice
2 bottles (16 oz. each) low-calorie
    lemon-lime carbonated beverage,
    chilled

In saucepan, combine water, cinnamon, and cloves.
Cover and simmer 15 minutes. Remove from heat and
strain into a large pitcher. Cool. Add Equal® and fruit
juices; chill. Just before serving, pour into large punch
bowl; slowly pour in lemon-lime carbonated beverage.
Serve over ice cubes.

Makes 24 servings.
Calories per serving: 40.
Diabetic exchanges per serving: milk 0,
    vegetable 0, fruit ½, bread 0, meat 0, fat 0.

Strawberry Punch

3 packages (10 oz. each) frozen, un-
    sweetened strawberries, thawed
2 bottles (24 oz. each) white grape
    juice, chilled
1 bottle (28 oz.) carbonated water,
    chilled
4 packets Equal®

Place 2 packages of the strawberries in a blender container. Cover and blend until smooth. In large pitcher
or punch bowl, combine blended berries, grape juice,

and remaining package of berries. Add Equal®. To
serve, add the chilled carbonated water; stir gently to
mix.

> *Makes 25 servings.*
> *Calories per serving: 50.*
> *Diabetic exchanges per serving: milk 0,*
>   *vegetable 0, fruit 1, bread 0, meat 0, fat 0.*

Ruby Lemon Punch

> **1 can (6 oz.) frozen lemonade concen-**
>   **trate, thawed**
> **4 cups low-calorie cranberry juice**
>   **cocktail**
> **1 bottle (16 oz.) low-calorie lemon-**
>   **lime carbonated beverage**
> **Ice cubes**
> **4 packets Equal®**
> **8 thin lemon slices (optional)**

Stir lemonade concentrate into cranberry juice cocktail. Slowly add carbonated beverage; stir gently with
an up and down motion. Add Equal®. Serve over ice.
Garnish with lemon slices if desired.

> *Makes 8 servings.*
> *Calories per serving: 67.*
> *Diabetic exchanges per serving: milk 0,*
>   *vegetable 0, fruit 1, bread 0, meat 0, fat 0.*

Sauces, Toppings, and Fillings

Almost any dessert—especially the simpler ones such as ice cream, uniced cake, or fruit—gains instant glamour when a creative sauce or topping is added as the finishing touch. Great taste and visual appeal can be provided at a fraction of the traditional calorie count.

Cornstarch is the thickening agent used in many of these sauces because it is lower in calories than flour. Cornstarch will also make your sauce glisten. Last-course favorites can be last-minute ones, too. Using these recipes will let you offer a first-class selection of desserts that you can make in record time without the hassle of complicated steps.

Tips for Successful Sauces, Toppings, and Fillings

- Dissolve cornstarch correctly in a small amount of cold water or juice before adding it to the sauce.
- Stir the sauce constantly when it is on the stove or it will stick and scorch on the bottom of the pan.
- Add extracts, flavorings, and Equal® after the sauce is removed from the stove.
- Be sure the sauce is thoroughly cooled before you store it in an airtight container for later use. If you cover the sauce while it is still hot, condensed moisture in the container will thin out the sauce.

Let your imagination be your guide. These recipes can be used on waffles, pancakes, fruits, custards, and angel food cake, taking a simple dessert to greater heights.

This basic sauce adds versatility and color to the simplest desserts.

Classic Light Fruit Sauce ♥

> 3 cups fresh berries; or 1¼–1½
> pounds of other fruit such as
> peaches and pears.
> 7 packets Equal®
> 1 or 2 teaspoons fresh lemon or or-
> ange juice; or 1 to 2 teaspoons
> flavored brandy or liqueur

Puree fruit in processor or blender. Strain sauce through fine sieve, pressing to extract as much liquid as possible. Whisk in 7 packets of Equal®. Cover and refrigerate at least 30 minutes. (Can be prepared 1 day ahead.) Stir in juice, brandy, or liqueur to taste, just before serving, if desired. Makes about 1 cup.

> *Makes 8 (2-tablespoon) servings.*
> *Calories per serving: 21.*
> *Diabetic exchanges per serving: milk 0,*
>   *vegetable 0, fruit 0, bread 0, meat 0, fat 0.*

Strawberry Topping ♥

> 3 cups unsweetened strawberries,
>   fresh or frozen
> ½ envelope (1½ teaspoons) unfla-
>   vored gelatin
> 1½ teaspoons lemon juice
> 4 packets Equal®

Put the strawberries in a saucepan. Cook, covered, over low heat without water for about 10 minutes. Remove the lid and bring fruit to the boiling point. Boil for 1 minute and remove from heat. Soften the gelatin in lemon juice. Pour some of the hot juice from the strawberries into the gelatin. Stir until the gelatin is completely dissolved. Add Equal® and the dissolved gelatin to the strawberries. Cool, then refrigerate. Makes 1¼ cups.

You can adapt this recipe for any fresh fruit topping, especially berries. Leftovers are great on crepes and puddings. Makes 1¼ cups.

Makes 12 (2-tablespoon) servings.
Calories per serving: 14.
Diabetic exchanges per serving: milk 0,
    vegetable 0, fruit 0, bread 0, meat 0, fat 0.

Pineapple Filling

1 can (8 oz.) unsweetened, crushed
    pineapple
3 tablespoons cornstarch
2 egg yolks, slightly beaten
6 packets Equal®

Drain pineapple, reserving liquid. Add water to reserved liquid to make ¾ cup. Place cornstarch in a small saucepan, stir in liquid, and mix well. Place mixture over medium heat and stir until it boils. Boil 1 minute. Blend small amount of hot mixture into egg yolks; then return it to saucepan. Mix well. Stir in pineapple and continue cooking until mixture begins to thicken, stirring constantly. Remove from heat, add Equal®, cool, and refrigerate. Makes 1½ cups.

Makes 12 (2-tablespoon) servings.
Calories per serving: 20.
Diabetic exchanges per serving: milk 0,
    vegetable 0, fruit 0, bread 0, meat 0, fat 0.

Vanilla Rum Sauce

2 beaten eggs
Dash salt
1 can (12 oz.) evaporated skim milk
½ teaspoon vanilla
¼ teaspoon rum extract
2 packets Equal®

In a heavy saucepan, combine eggs and milk. Cook and stir over medium-low heat till mixture coats a metal spoon. Remove from heat; cool slightly. Stir in vanilla, rum extract, and Equal®. Cover and chill.

To serve, spoon 3 tablespoons sauce over desired fruit in individual serving dish. Serve immediately. Refrigerate remaining sauce for up to 4 days.

Makes 9 (3-tablespoon) servings.
Calories per serving: 48.
Diabetic exchanges per serving: milk ½,
  vegetable 0, fruit 0, bread 0, meat 0, fat 0.

Kiwi Topping

½ cup unsweetened apple juice
2 tablespoons melon-flavored liqueur
1 teaspoon cornstarch
⅔ cup peeled, sliced kiwi fruit
2 packets Equal®

Combine first 3 ingredients in a small, non-aluminum saucepan; stir well. Bring to a boil over medium heat, stirring constantly; cook 1 minute, stirring constantly. Remove from heat; stir in kiwi fruit. Stir in Equal®. Cool completely. Serve over frozen, low-fat yogurt or angel food cake. Makes 1 cup.

Makes 4 (¼-cup) servings.
Calories per serving: 76.
Diabetic exchanges per serving: milk 0,
  vegetable 0, fruit 1, bread 0, meat 0, fat 0.

Rum Custard Sauce

> 1 cup skim milk
> 1 cup half-and-half
> 4 extra-large egg yolks
> Pinch of salt
> 1 teaspoon vanilla extract
> 10 packets Equal®
> 2 tablespoons rum

In a heavy saucepan, scald the milk and half-and-half. While the milk is scalding, in a mixing bowl beat egg yolks and salt until thick and pale. Slowly pour scalded liquid into the yolk mixture, stirring constantly. Return mixture to saucepan and cook over low heat, stirring constantly with a wooden spoon until the sauce is just thick enough to lightly coat the back of the spoon. Immediately pour the sauce into a clean bowl. Stir in vanilla, Equal®, and rum. Refrigerate—tightly covered—up to 1 week. Makes about 2½ cups.

Makes 10 (¼-cup) servings.
Calories per serving: 77.
Diabetic exchanges per serving: milk 0,
    vegetable 0, fruit 0, bread 0, meat 0, fat 2.

Bourbon Sauce

> 1 teaspoon cornstarch
> 1 cup milk
> ½ teaspoon vanilla
> 3 egg yolks
> 2 tablespoons bourbon whiskey
> 3 packets Equal®

Dissolve cornstarch in 2 tablespoons milk. Scald remaining milk and vanilla in heavy, small saucepan. Whisk cornstarch mixture into milk. Whisk the yolks in a bowl until thick and pale. Gradually, whisk in milk mixture. Whisk everything back into saucepan, and stir

over medium heat until sauce thickens enough to coat
the back of a spoon. *Do not boil.* Remove from heat. Stir
in bourbon and Equal®. Makes about 1½ cups.

Makes 6 (¼-cup) servings.
Calories per serving: 63.
Diabetic exchanges per serving: milk 0,
    vegetable 0, fruit 0, bread 0, meat 0, fat 1½.

Raspberry Sauce ♥

2 packages (10 oz. each) frozen, un-
sweetened raspberries, thawed
2 teaspoons cornstarch
8 packets Equal®

Place one package of raspberries in container of
blender and blend until liquified. Place liquified berries
and cornstarch in a small, non-aluminum saucepan,
stirring with a wire whisk until well blended. Bring to a
boil; cook over medium heat, stirring constantly, until
thickened. Remove from heat. Stir in the other package
of whole berries and Equal®. Cover and chill. Makes 2
cups.

Makes 8 (¼-cup) servings.
Calories per serving: 42.
Diabetic exchanges per serving: milk 0,
    vegetable 0, fruit ½, bread 0, meat 0, fat 0.

Vanilla Sauce

1 egg
3 tablespoons flour
¼ teaspoon salt
1¼ cups skim milk
10 packets Equal®
1 teaspoon vanilla extract

Beat egg lightly and set aside. Combine flour and salt in a small saucepan. Gradually add milk, stirring well. Cook and stir over medium heat until mixture boils. Boil 1 minute. Blend a small amount of the hot mixture into beaten egg; then add egg mixture to saucepan. Stir well. Continue cooking until mixture thickens, stirring constantly. Remove from heat; stir in Equal® and vanilla. Cool and refrigerate. Makes 1½ cups.

6 (¼-cup) servings.
Calories per serving: 52.
Diabetic exchanges per serving: milk ½,
    vegetable 0, fruit 0, bread 0, meat 0, fat 0.

Fudge Sauce ♥

2 cups skim milk
1 tablespoon cocoa powder
¼ teaspoon chocolate extract
2 teaspoons cornstarch
1 square (1 oz.) unsweetened baking
    chocolate
6 packets Equal®

Mix all ingredients, except chocolate and Equal®, stirring to remove the lumps. When smooth, place over low heat and stir in chocolate. Cook until mixture thickens. Remove from heat and add Equal®. Makes 2 cups.

This sauce is excellent served over vanilla yogurt or used as a dip for fresh fruit.

Makes 16 (2-tablespoon) servings.
Calories per serving: 23.
Diabetic exchanges per serving: milk 0,
    vegetable 0, fruit 0, bread 0, meat 0, fat 0.

Custard Sauce ♥

3 eggs
8 packets Equal®
2½ cups skim milk
1 teaspoon vanilla extract

Beat eggs briefly. Put eggs in the top of a double boiler. Put hot water in the bottom of the double boiler, but do not let top pan touch water. Add milk slowly, stirring constantly, and cook over medium heat until mixture coats a metal spoon. Water in double boiler should not boil. Remove top of double boiler from heat, and stir vanilla and Equal® into the custard. Place top of double boiler in cold water until custard cools. Cover and chill for several hours. Makes 3 cups.

Custard sauce is excellent over miniature cream puffs or sponge cake.

Makes 12 (¼-cup) servings.
Calories per serving: 81.
Diabetic exchanges per serving: milk ½,
   vegetable 0, fruit 0, bread 0, meat 0, fat ½.

Fruit Desserts

Fruit is the dieter's best friend because it's nutritious and mostly low-calorie. Fruit also helps to make you feel full due to its high fiber content. Fruit is also loaded with vitamins and energy-packed carbohydrates.

We are fortunate to live in a country where fruit is available in the markets during every month of the year. Add to all that the natural sweetness it imparts to desserts and you have a near-perfect diet food. While some fruits are almost always available, each fruit has a special season when flavor is at its peak. Fortunately, when fruit is in season, it is also least expensive.

Light, yet satisfying, beautiful to look at fruit desserts can be elegant or simple. In this chapter you will find recipes for both, such as bananas flambé, peach-blueberry cobbler, and strawberries Romanoff. Let your imagination soar, and you will create some interesting combinations of your own.

Tips for Successful Fruit Desserts

- Always purchase ripe fruit close to the time you're planning to use it.
- Be sure that packaged and frozen fruits are unsweetened.
- To facilitate cutting sticky foods, such as dried fruits, dip the knife into hot water.
- Be sure to dip cut bananas in lemon juice to prevent discoloration.

Cranberry-Orange Dip and Fruit

>   1 carton (8 oz.) orange low-fat yogurt
>   ½ cup cranberry-orange relish
>   ¼ teaspoon ground nutmeg
>   ¼ teaspoon ground ginger
>   1 medium apple
>   1 medium nectarine
>   1 tablespoon lemon juice
>   1 cup seedless grapes
>   1 cup strawberries
>   1 cup fresh pineapple cut into chunks
>   1 medium banana cut into chunks
>   3 packets Equal®
>   Lettuce leaves

Combine yogurt, relish, nutmeg, and ginger. Cover and chill. Just before serving, core apple and remove pit from nectarine. Slice apple and nectarine; brush with lemon juice.

Place all the fruit in a bowl and sprinkle with Equal®. Arrange lettuce leaves on a platter and top with fruit. Serve dip alongside in a bowl, with picks for easy handling.

> *Makes 10 servings.*
> *Calories per serving: 92.*
> *Diabetic exchanges per serving: milk 0,*
>   *vegetable 0, fruit 1½, bread 0, meat 0, fat 0.*

Blushing Peaches ♥

>   1 cup dry red wine
>   Zest of ½ orange
>   8 large peaches
>   3 packets Equal®
>   Whipped dessert topping (optional)

Combine wine and orange zest in a small saucepan. Bring to a boil and remove from heat. Place peaches in a large pan and cover with boiling water; let stand a couple of minutes; drain; plunge into cold water. Peel, halve, and pit peaches. Drop peach halves into wine and return saucepan to moderate heat; bring to boil and lower heat. Simmer 5 to 10 minutes or until peaches are tender. Remove from heat. Stir in Equal®. Using a slotted spoon, remove peach halves and place the peaches in a glass serving dish. Distribute liquid evenly among the dishes. Garnish with a dollop of whipped dessert topping if desired.

Makes 8 servings.
Calories per serving: 60.
Diabetic exchanges per serving: milk 0,
    vegetable 0, fruit 1, bread 0, meat 0, fat 0.

Fresh Fruit Hawaiian ♥

1 cup fresh pineapple chunks
1 papaya, peeled, seeded, and cubed
½ cup sliced fresh strawberries
1 kiwi fruit, peeled and sliced
1 teaspoon lime juice
2 packets Equal®

Combine pineapple, papaya, strawberries, kiwi fruit, and lime juice. Sprinkle with Equal® and lime juice. Chill thoroughly.

Makes 4 servings.
Calories per serving: 52.
Diabetic exchanges per serving: milk 0,
    vegetable 0, fruit 1, bread 0, meat 0, fat 0.

Fruit and Yogurt Sensation

> 3 egg yolks
> ¼ cup water
> 1 teaspoon cornstarch
> 2 cartons (8 oz. each) plain yogurt
> 6 packets Equal®
> 2 cups sliced fresh strawberries
> 2 cups cantaloupe or honeydew
>   melon balls
> 2 cups seedless grapes, halved
> 2 kiwi fruit, peeled and sliced
> 2 cups banana, sliced
> 2 tablespoons lemon and lime zest

In a small saucepan, combine egg yolks, water, and cornstarch; mix well. Cook and stir over medium heat till mixture comes to a boil. Reduce heat; cook and stir 2 minutes longer. Spoon mixture into a small bowl. Without stirring, cover and chill several hours. At serving time, fold yolk mixture into yogurt, add Equal®, and blend well. In a large brandy snifter or individual parfait glasses, layer fruit and yogurt mixture, ending with yogurt on top. Sprinkle with lemon and lime zest.

Makes 10 servings.
Calories per serving: 136.
Diabetic exchanges per serving: milk 0,
*   vegetable 0, fruit 1½, bread 0, meat 0, fat 1.*

Fruit and Cheese Surprise

> 1 package (6 oz.) lemon-flavored
>   gelatin
> 2 cups boiling water
> 1 cup dry white wine
> 1 cup plain yogurt
> 2 packets Equal®

2 cups assorted fresh fruits, such as
    melon balls*, strawberries, peaches,
    blueberries, or seedless grapes,
    halved
½ cup shredded Monterey Jack
    cheese
Fruit sauce (page 33), optional

Dissolve gelatin in boiling water; stir in wine. Gradually beat gelatin mixture into yogurt. Add Equal® and
stir well. Chill till partially set (consistency of unbeaten
egg whites). Fold in fruit and cheese. Turn mixture into
a 5½- or 6-cup mold. Chill several hours or overnight.
Unmold to serve by dipping mold into warm water and
inverting it onto a platter.

Can be garnished with fruit sauce if desired.

Makes 8 servings.
Calories per serving: 120.
Diabetic exchanges per serving: milk 0,
    vegetable 0, fruit ½, bread 0, meat 1, fat 0.

*Do not use watermelon in this recipe.

Bananas Flambé

4 small bananas (about 1¾ pounds)
1 tablespoon lemon juice
2 tablespoons diet margarine
2 packets Equal®
¼ teaspoon cinnamon
¼ cup rum

Cut bananas in half crosswise, then lengthwise. Toss
with lemon juice; set aside. Place margarine in a large
skillet. Add bananas and cook over medium heat, stirring constantly, for about 4 minutes, turning once.
Sprinkle with cinnamon and remove from heat. Stir in
Equal® and mix well. Pour rum over banana mixture.
Ignite rum with a long match; let flames die down.

Makes 8 servings.
Calories per serving: 87.
Diabetic exchanges per serving: milk 0,
   vegetable 0, fruit 0, bread 1, meat 0, fat 0.

No-Cook Applesauce ♥

> **4 medium apples, peeled, quartered,**
>   **and cored**
> **½ medium orange, chopped with**
>   **peel**
> **¼ cup water**
> **1 tablespoon lemon juice**
> **6 packets Equal®**
> **Dash of cinnamon**

Slice apples into container of blender or food processor. Add orange, water, and lemon juice. Cover and blend till almost smooth. Add Equal® and continue to blend till smooth. Spoon into dessert dishes, and sprinkle each serving lightly with cinnamon.

> *Makes 4 servings.*
> *Calories per serving: 95.*
> *Diabetic exchanges per serving: milk 0,*
>   *vegetable 0, fruit 1½, bread 0, meat 0, fat 0.*

Fresh Fruit Dazzler

> **3 ounces Neufchâtel cheese, softened**
> **⅔ cup raspberry yogurt**
> **2¼ cups fresh whole strawberries**
> **2 small oranges, sectioned**
> **1 cup fresh raspberries**
> **2 small bananas**
> **5 packets Equal®**

In small mixer bowl, beat cheese till fluffy. Add half of the yogurt; beat till smooth. Stir in remaining yogurt. Cover and chill. Halve strawberries, combine with oranges, raspberries, and bananas. Sprinkle with Equal®. Chill. To serve, spoon ½ cup of the fruit into each of 8 dessert dishes. Spoon yogurt mixture on top.

Makes 8 servings.
Calories per serving: 113.
Diabetic exchanges per serving: milk 0,
    vegetable 0, fruit 1½, bread 0, meat 0, fat ½.

Green 'n Gold Delight ♥

1 1¼-pound can water-packed pineapple chunks
2 cups cantaloupe balls
1 cup seedless green grapes, halved
2 kiwi fruit, peeled and sliced
8 packets Equal®
4 teaspoons shredded orange peel
1 cup low-calorie lemon-lime carbonated beverage, chilled

Drain pineapple chunks, reserving liquid. Combine pineapple, melon, grapes, kiwi fruit, and Equal® in a bowl and stir well. Chill thoroughly. Just before serving, sprinkle orange peel over fruit and pour lemon-lime beverage along the outer sides of bowl. Place fruit in dessert cups, and ladle carbonated beverage over top.

Makes 5 servings.
Calories per serving: 96.
Diabetic exchanges per serving: milk 0,
    vegetable 0, fruit 1½, bread 0, meat 0, fat 0.

Peach Clafouti

1½ cups peeled peach slices
⅓ cup milk
⅓ cup half-and-half
1 egg, room temperature
2 tablespoons all-purpose flour
½ teaspoon vanilla
5 packets Equal®
Diet whipped topping (optional)

Preheat oven to 375°. Spray two 8-oz. au gratin dishes or one small baking dish with vegetable cooking spray. Arrange peaches in single layer in dish(es). Mix milk, half-and-half, egg, flour, and vanilla until smooth. Pour batter over peaches. Bake clafouti until puffed and golden, 35 to 40 minutes. Remove from oven and sprinkle with Equal®.
Garnish with whipped topping if desired.

Makes 2 servings.
Calories per serving: 197.
Diabetic exchanges per serving: milk 0,
*   vegetable 0, fruit 1, bread ½, meat ½, fat 1.*

Apple and Pear Crisp

1½ pounds apples and pears, peeled,
    cored, thinly sliced
3 tablespoons flour
¼ cup frozen, unsweetened apple
    juice concentrate
½ teaspoon cinnamon
Dash freshly ground nutmeg
3 tablespoons diet margarine,
    softened
10 graham cracker squares, crushed
    (¾ cup)
8 packets Equal®

Heat oven to 375° degrees. In an 8-in. square baking dish, toss the apples and pears with 1 tablespoon of the flour. Add the concentrated apple juice. Coat well. In a small bowl, combine the remaining 2 tablespoons of flour and the spices with the margarine and mix until well blended. Gradually, stir in graham cracker crumbs until mixture resembles coarse crumbs. Sprinkle evenly over the fruit. Bake for 30 minutes, or until the topping is lightly browned and the fruit is tender. Remove from the oven and sprinkle with Equal®.

Makes 8 (4-inch square) servings.
Calories per serving: 121.
Diabetic exchanges per serving: milk 0,
    vegetable 0, fruit 1, bread ½, meat 0, fat ½.

Apple Delight ♥

4 cups peeled, sliced Delicious apples
    (Golden if available)
½ cup flour
½ teaspoon cinnamon
¼ teaspoon nutmeg
¼ cup chopped walnuts
½ cup diet margarine
8 packets Equal®
Diet whipped topping

Place apple slices in the bottom of a greased baking dish. In a mixing bowl, combine flour and spices. Cut in shortening until crumbly. Add walnuts. Bake for 30 to 40 mintues at 375°. Remove from oven. Sprinkle Equal® on top. Serve with whipped topping.

Makes 4 servings.
Calories per serving: 246.
Diabetic exchanges per serving: milk 0,
    vegetable 0, fruit 1, bread 1, meat 0, fat 2.

Marsala Baked Apples

    1 tablespoon golden raisins
    1 tablespoon currants
    4 teaspoons toasted pine nuts or sliv-
        ered toasted almonds
    Grated peel of 1 large lemon
    4 medium Rome Beauty apples, cored
    4 tablespoons Marsala wine
    1 cup boiling water
    2 tablespoons fresh lemon juice
    2 teaspoons sugar

Preheat oven to 325°. Mix raisins, currants, pine nuts, and lemon peel. Fill apples evenly with mixture. Cut a thin slit horizontally around middle of each apple to prevent bursting while cooking. Arrange apples upright in baking dish just large enough to hold fruit snugly. Drizzle 1 tablespoon Marsala into each filled hollow.

Combine water and lemon juice, and pour mixture over apples. Cover apples with foil. Bake until tender, about 1 hour. Discard foil. Continue baking for about 20 minutes until apples are very soft and golden brown, basting frequently. If raisins begin to brown, cover filling with a little piece of foil.

Transfer apples to dessert plates. Spoon juices remaining in baking dish on each apple. Sprinkle one packet of Equal® over each apple. Serve warm.

Makes 4 servings.
Calories per serving: 128.
Diabetic exchanges per serving: milk 0,
    vegetable 0, fruit 2, bread 0, meat 0, fat 0.

Mocha Strawberries

    12 medium-large strawberries
    3 packets Equal®
    1 ounce semisweet chocolate, coarsely
        chopped
    1½ teaspoons brewed coffee
    1 teaspoon coffee liqueur

Place strawberries in bowl. Sprinkle with Equal®. Melt chocolate with coffee and liqueur in double boiler over gently simmering water. Stir until smooth. Dip bottom half of strawberries in chocolate. Arrange stems up on aluminum foil. Refrigerate until chocolate is set. These are lovely served on a small glass plate lined with a pretty doily. The strawberries can be prepared 1 day ahead and refrigerated.

Makes 4 servings of 3 berries each.
Calories per serving: 60.
Diabetic exchanges per serving: milk 0,
*   vegetable 0, fruit ½, bread 0, meat 0, fat 1.*

Summer Fruit Compote ♥

½ cup frozen orange juice concen-
    trate, thawed and undiluted
2 tablespoons chopped candied ginger
2 medium-size plums, sliced
1 medium-size peach, sliced
1 medium-size nectarine, sliced
1 medium Bartlett pear, sliced
3 packets Equal®

In small, non-aluminum bowl, combine juice concentrate and ginger and mix well. In serving bowl, arrange fruit; sprinkle with Equal®. Pour ginger sauce over fruit and mix well. Cover and chill. Toss gently before serving to distribute sauce.

Makes 4 servings.
Calories per serving: 90.
Diabetic exchanges per serving: milk 0,
*   vegetable 0, fruit 1½, bread 0, meat 0, fat 0.*

French Apple Wedges ♥ (Microwave)

¼ teaspoon ground cinnamon
⅛ teaspoon ground ginger
⅛ teaspoon ground cloves
1 large, unpeeled red cooking apple,
   cored and cut into 8 wedges
2 packets Equal®

Combine first 3 ingredients in a small bowl; stir well.
Press cut sides of apple in spice mixture. Place 4
wedges on a large, heavy-duty paper plate. Cover with
wax paper, and microwave at high setting for 45 seconds or until thoroughly heated. Repeat procedure
with remaining wedges. Remove from microwave and
sprinkle one packet of Equal® on both sides of apples
on each plate.

Makes 2 servings.
Calories per serving: 45.
Diabetic exchanges per serving: milk 0,
   vegetable 0, fruit 1, bread 0, meat 0, fat 0.

Melon Balls with Ginger Sauce

⅔ cup white grape juice
2 teaspoons cornstarch
2 teaspoons chopped, crystallized
   ginger
2 tablespoons dry sherry
½ medium cantaloupe, peeled and
   cut into chunks
2 cups casaba melon balls
2 cups honeydew melon balls
2 packets Equal®
Lemon rind, grated

In a medium saucepan, combine grape juice, cornstarch and crystallized ginger. Cook and stir till thickened and bubbly. Cook and stir 1 to 2 minutes more.
Stir in sherry.

To serve, arrange melon chunks and balls on individual dessert plates. Add Equal® to sauce and drizzle hot sauce over fruit.

Garnish with finely-grated lime rind.

Makes 4 servings.
Calories per serving: 105.
Diabetic exchanges per serving: milk 0,
*   vegetable 0, fruit 1½, bread 0, meat 0, fat 0.*

Caribbean Fruit Salad ♥

1 can (14 oz.) hearts of palm, drained
    and sliced
1 medium banana, quartered
1 medium papaya, seeded, peeled,
    and sliced
1 large orange, peeled and sectioned
2 tablespoons lemon juice
2 tablespoons lime juice
1 tablespoon vegetable cooking oil
⅛ teaspoon ground cinnamon
⅛ teaspoon paprika
5 packets Equal®
Lettuce leaves
5 tablespoons unsweetened, grated
    coconut

In a medium mixing bowl, combine the hearts of palm, banana, papaya, and orange sections.

For dressing, in a screw-top jar combine the lemon juice, lime juice, cooking oil, Equal®, cinnamon, and paprika. Cover and shake well to mix.

Pour dressing over fruit mixture; toss gently to coat. Arrange fruit on a lettuce-lined platter or individual salad plates. Sprinkle coconut over the fruit salad.

Makes 4 servings.
Calories per serving: 165.
Diabetic exchanges per serving: milk 0,
*   vegetable 2, fruit 1, bread 0, meat 0, fat 1.*

Peach-Blueberry Cobbler

1 tablespoon cornstarch
¾ cup orange juice
1½ cups fresh or frozen peach slices,
   thawed
1 cup fresh or frozen blueberries,
   thawed
½ cup all-purpose flour
½ cup whole-wheat flour
1½ teaspoons baking powder
⅓ cup skim milk
3 tablespoons cooking oil (vegetable)
8 packets Equal®

In a small saucepan, stir together cornstarch and orange juice. Cook and stir till bubbly. Add peaches and blueberries; cook till fruit is hot. Keep warm.

Stir together flours and baking powder. Add milk and oil; stir till mixture forms a ball. On floured surface, pat into an 8-in. circle. Cut into 8 wedges. Spoon hot berry mixture into a 9-in. pie plate; immediately top with the dough wedges.

Bake in 425° oven 25 to 30 minutes or till wedges are brown. Remove from oven and lift the pastry wedges off the berries. Gently stir in 4 packets of Equal®. Replace the pastry wedges and sprinkle with the 4 remaining packets of Equal®.

Makes 8 servings.
Calories per serving: 145.
Diabetic exchanges per serving: milk 0,
   vegetable 0, fruit ½, bread 1, meat 0, fat 1.

Strawberries Romanoff

1 pint fresh strawberries, washed,
   hulled, and sliced
2 packets Equal®

> 3 tablespoons plus 1 teaspoon Cointreau or other orange liqueur
> 1 envelope diet dessert topping mix
> 2 packets Equal®

Toss berries with 2 packets Equal®; let stand 5 minutes. Add 3 tablespoons liqueur. Beat cream with Equal® and 1 teaspoon liqueur until soft peaks form. Place strawberries in 4 long-stemmed glasses and ladle topping mix over them.

> *Makes 4 servings.*
> *Calories per serving: 60.*
> *Diabetic exchanges per serving: milk 0,*
>   *vegetable 0, fruit ½, bread 0, meat 0, fat 0.*

Glazed Pineapple ♥   (Microwave optional)

> 1 can (13½ oz.) unsweetened pineapple tidbits
> 1 tablespoon cornstarch
> ¼ teaspoon cinnamon
> 2 tablespoons diet margarine
> 3 packets Equal®

Conventional Method: Put pineapple in a 1-quart saucepan. Mix cornstarch and cinnamon and add to pineapple. Cut margarine into 2 pieces and add to pineapple. Cook over medium heat until pineapple is tender, approximately 15 minutes, stirring constantly. Remove from heat and stir in Equal®. Serve hot.

Microwave Method: Put pineapple in a 1-quart casserole. Mix cornstarch and cinnamon in a small bowl. Add to pineapple, stirring well. Cut margarine into 2 pieces and place over top. Cover. Microwave at high setting for 6–7 minutes, stirring well after 3 minutes. Remove from oven and stir in Equal®. Serve hot. Makes 1⅔ cups.

> *Makes 4 servings.*
> *Calories per serving: 70.*
> *Diabetic exchanges per serving: milk 0,*
>   *vegetable 0, fruit 1, bread 0, meat 0, fat 0.*

Pies

Pies are so versatile that it's easy to see why they are a big favorite. A light pastry shell can be filled with fruit, a frothy chiffon, custard, or a cheese filling. This chapter even includes the all-American dessert, Apple Pie.

If your diet does not allow for the calories in a pie crust, remember that pie fillings alone make excellent desserts. Spoon them into pretty dishes and you will have a delicious meal-finisher.

Tips for Successful Pies

- Pies that do not contain sugar may "weep," so they are best served the same day. If stored overnight, they may be a little watery.
- Prepare pie crusts first and set them aside while you make the filling. Pie crusts can be made in advance and frozen. This will allow you to make a pie on a moment's notice.
- Pastry freezes extremely well, either baked or unbaked. You can roll it out without chilling if it's going to be frozen, or you can freeze it in a ball and roll it out later.
- When "folding," slide your spatula across the bottom and up the sides of the bowl; then bring the spatula back down into the center of the mixture.
- Be sure that gelatin is the consistency of egg whites before you fold it into other ingredients.
- Don't fold still-warm gelatin into whipped ingredients such as whipped milk. The heat will deflate these volume-dependent ingredients.
- To avoid a tough skin on the surface of your pie, cover it with plastic wrap or aluminum foil.

Café au Lait Pie

Chocolate Crumb Crust (page 78)

Filling: 2 envelopes (2 tablespoons) unflavored gelatin
½ cup water
2½ cups skim milk
3 egg yolks
1 tablespoon instant coffee
½ teaspoon salt
4 packets Equal®
3 egg whites
1 teaspoon vanilla
¼ teaspoon cream of tartar
2 packets Equal®
Chocolate curls for garnish (optional)

Prepare Chocolate Crumb Crust and set aside.

Soften 2 envelopes of gelatin in ½ cup cold water. In medium saucepan, beat 2½ cups skim milk and 3 egg yolks. Add instant coffee, salt, and softened gelatin. Cook and stir till mixture thickens and gelatin is dissolved.

Remove from heat and stir in 4 packets Equal®. Chill till partially set. Beat 3 egg whites, 1 teaspoon vanilla, cream of tartar, and 2 packets of Equal® till soft peaks form. Fold in gelatin mixture. Spoon into pie shell and chill till firm. Garnish with chocolate curls if desired.

Makes one 8- or 9-inch pie.
Serves 8.
Calories per serving: 100.
Diabetic exchanges per serving: milk 1,
    vegetable 0, fruit 0, bread 0, meat 0, fat 0.

Cranberry Chiffon Pie

9-inch Graham Cracker Crust (page 79)

Filling: 2 tablespoons cornstarch
2 cups cranberry juice
1 envelope (1 tablespoon) unflavored gelatin
¼ teaspoon salt
3 packets Equal®
3 egg whites
1 cup frozen whipped topping, thawed
Orange rind, grated

Prepare Graham Cracker Crust and set aside.

Put cornstarch in small saucepan and dissolve it in a small amount of cranberry juice. Add remaining juice, gelatin, and salt. Cook and stir over medium heat until mixture thickens and bubbles. Remove from heat and stir in Equal®. Pour cranberry mixture into a bowl. Chill, stirring frequently, until mixture mounds slightly when dropped from a spoon. Beat egg whites until stiff peaks form. Fold in cranberry mixture, then whipped topping. Pour into prepared crust. Refrigerate until firm.

Garnish this pie with whipped topping and grated orange rind.

Makes one 8- or 9-inch pie.
Serves 8.
Calories per serving: 165.
Diabetic exchanges per serving: milk 0,
vegetable 0, fruit ½, bread 1, meat 0, fat 1.

Sherry Pie

Chocolate Crumb Crust (page 78)

Filling: **1 envelope unflavored gelatin
¼ cup cold water
4 eggs, separated
½ cup sherry (not cooking sherry)
8 packets Equal®**

Prepare Chocolate Crumb Crust and set aside.

Stir gelatin into cold water. Beat egg yolks slightly in small saucepan and cook over low heat, stirring constantly, 5 minutes. Add gelatin and stir until mixture is slightly thickened and gelatin dissolves. Remove from heat. Stir in 6 packets of Equal® and sherry. Chill in refrigerator until mixture mounds slightly when dropped from a spoon, about 15 minutes. Beat egg whites until frothy. Add 2 packets of Equal®, and keep beating until stiff peaks form. Spread over gelatin; fold in egg whites. Spoon into pastry shell; chill until firm.

Makes one 9-inch pie.
Serves 8.
Calories per serving: 101.
Diabetic exchanges per serving: milk 0,
    vegetable 0, fruit 0, bread ½, meat 0, fat 1.

Chocolate Mousse Pie

Chocolate Crumb Crust (page 78)

Filling: **1 teaspoon unflavored gelatin
1 tablespoon cold water
2 tablespoons boiling water
¼ cup cocoa
1 cup heavy cream, well chilled
1 teaspoon vanilla
10 packets Equal®
Cool Whip (optional)**

Prepare Chocolate Crumb Crust and set aside.

Sprinkle gelatin into cold water in small bowl; let stand 1 minute to soften. Add boiling water; stir until gelatin is completely dissolved and mixture is clear. Put cocoa in chilled, small mixer bowl; add cream and vanilla. Beat 30 seconds on low speed or until smooth; beat 1 minute on medium speed or until stiff peaks form. Add 10 packets of Equal® and stir well. Gradually, add gelatin mixture; beat until blended. Pour into pie shell and chill to set.

Garnish with a dollup of Cool Whip if desired.

Makes one 8- or 9-inch pie.
Serves 8.
Calories per serving: 160.
Diabetic exchanges per serving: milk 0,
    vegetable 0, fruit 0, bread 1, meat 0, fat 2.

Individual Cherry Tarts

Crusts: **2¼ cups sifted all-purpose flour**
         1 teaspoon salt
         ¾ cup solid vegetable shortening
         6 tablespoons ice water

Filling: **1 can (16 oz.) tart cherries in water,**
             drained (liquid reserved)
          2 tablespoons cornstarch
          ¼ teaspoon salt
          2 tablespoons diet margarine
          8 packets Equal®
          Whipped cream (optional)

To Make Crusts: Preheat oven to 400°. Lightly butter outside of 12 muffin cups. Combine flour and salt in medium bowl. Cut in shortening, using pastry blender or 2 knives until mixture resembles coarse meal. Set ⅔ of the dough aside. Add ice water to remaining ⅓ and blend well. Return reserved dough to bowl and mix well.

Gather pastry into a ball. Roll out on lightly-floured surface to thickness of ⅛ inch. Cut out 12 circles, using 3½-inch cutter. Mold circles around the outside of prepared muffin cups. Prick pastry shells with fork. Bake until lightly browned, about 25 minutes. Cool crust briefly on cups; then carefully remove cups and transfer crusts to rack to cool completely.

To Make Filling: Heat reserved liquid from cherries in medium saucepan over medium heat. Add cornstarch and salt. Cook just until thickened, clear, and smooth, about 4 to 5 minutes. Remove from heat. Add cherries and margarine and mix well. Stir in Equal®. Cool to room temperature. Spoon into crusts; top with whipped cream. Refrigerate.

> *Makes 12 tarts.*
> *Calories per tart: 200.*
> *Diabetic exchanges per tart: milk 0, vegetable*
> * 0, fruit ½, bread 1, meat 0, fat 2.*

Slim Lemon Pie

9-inch Graham Cracker Crust (page 79)

Filling: **1 envelope unflavored gelatin**
½ cup water
1½ cups (12 oz.) lemon yogurt
6 packets Equal®
1 teaspoon grated lemon peel
Yellow food coloring, optional
⅓ cup nonfat dry milk
⅓ cup ice water
1 tablespoon lemon juice
Lemon and lime slices

Prepare Graham Cracker Crust and set aside.
In a small saucepan, sprinkle gelatin over water; cook over low heat until gelatin dissolves. Cool slightly. In medium-size bowl, combine yogurt, Equal®, lemon

peel, and food coloring; stir in gelatin mixture. Chill until mixture mounds when dropped from spoon, about 30 minutes. In small bowl, combine nonfat dry milk, ice water, and lemon juice; beat on high speed until stiff peaks form, about 5 minutes. Fold into gelatin-yogurt mixture. Spoon filling into Graham Cracker Crust. Refrigerate until set, about 3 hours or overnight. Garnish with lemon and lime slices.

Makes one 9-inch pie.
Serves 8.
Calories per serving: 140.
Diabetic exchanges per serving: milk 0,
   vegetable 0, fruit 0, bread 1, meat 0, fat 1.

Chocolate Coconut Tart

Chocolate Crumb Crust (page 78)

Filling: **3 tablespoons unsweetened cocoa**
3 tablespoons cornstarch
2 cups skim milk
5 packets Equal®
1 teaspoon vanilla extract
**½ cup frozen, non-dairy whipped
   topping, thawed**
½ cup grated, unsweetened coconut

Prepare Chocolate Crumb Crust and set aside.

In medium-size saucepan over medium heat, combine cocoa and cornstarch; gradually stir in milk. Cook, stirring constantly, until mixture boils; boil 1 minute, stirring constantly. Remove from heat and stir in Equal® and vanilla.

Cool slightly. Pour into Chocolate Crumb Crust; press plastic wrap over filling and chill at least 2 hours. Remove plastic wrap. Spread whipped topping over tart, starting in the center and working outward. Sprinkle coconut over whipped topping and outer edges of tart.

Serves 10.
Calories per serving: 96.
Diabetic exchanges per serving: milk 0,
    vegetable 0, fruit 1, bread 0, meat 0, fat 1.

Fresh Peach Pie ♥   (Microwave optional)

8- or 9-inch baked Pie Crust (page 77)

Filling: **5 cups sliced, fresh peaches**
            1 tablespoon lemon juice
            3 tablespoons quick-cooking tapioca
            ½ teaspoon ground coriander or
                cinnamon
            10 packets Equal®

Prepare Pie Crust and set aside. Then proceed with one of these two methods.

Conventional Method: Place sliced peaches in a medium saucepan. Stir in lemon juice. Add tapioca and cinnamon; stir gently and allow to stand 10 minutes. Cook and stir over medium heat until mixture is bubbly and peaches are tender when pierced. Let cool 1 hour, then add Equal® and spoon into baked pie crust.

Microwave Method: Place sliced peaches in a glass baking dish. Stir in lemon juice. Combine tapioca and cinnamon; stir gently into peach slices. Allow peaches to stand about 10 minutes. Microwave on high setting, uncovered, 13 minutes or until mixture is bubbly and peaches are tender when pierced; stir 5 or 6 times while cooking. Let cool about 1 hour, then add Equal® and spoon into baked pie crust.

Makes one 8- or 9-inch pie.
Serves 8.
Calories per serving: 235.
Diabetic exchanges per serving: milk 0,
    vegetable 0, fruit 1, bread 1, meat 0, fat 2.

Orange Pie

1⅓ cup flaked, unsweetened coconut
(1, 3½-oz. can)
1 tablespoon diet margarine
1 can (20 oz.) crushed pineapple
(juice pack)
1 envelope unflavored gelatin
2 cartons (8 oz. each) orange low-fat
yogurt
2 packets Equal®

Place 1¼ cups of coconut in a bowl; toss with melted margarine. Press on the bottom and up sides of a 9-in. pie plate. Bake in a 325° oven about 15 minutes or until golden. Cool on wire rack. Place remaining coconut in a shallow pan and toast in 325° oven about 1 minute. Set aside.

Drain pineapple, reserving juice. Set fruit aside. Add water, if necessary, to reserved juice to make ¾ cup liquid. In small saucepan, soften gelatin in the pineapple liquid. Cook and stir over low heat till gelatin is dissolved. Chill till partially set (consistency of unbeaten egg whites). Beat partially-set gelatin mixture till fluffy. Fold in yogurt and Equal® and drained pineapple. Pile into crust. Toast the reserved coconut and use as garnish.

Makes one 9-inch pie.
Serves 8.
Calories per serving: 170.
Diabetic exchanges per serving: milk 0,
    vegetable 0, fruit 1, bread 1, meat 0, fat 1.

Apple Pie

8- or 9- inch baked Pie Crust (page 77)

Filling: 2 tablespoons diet margarine
6 cups peeled, sliced Delicious apples
⅝ cup water
2 tablespoons cornstarch
1 teaspoon cinnamon
⅛ teaspoon nutmeg
6 packets Equal®

Prepare Pie Crust and set aside.
Melt margarine in heavy saucepan. Add apples and
½ cup water. Bring to a boil. Cover. Reduce heat and
simmer, stirring occasionally, until apples are tender.
Add spices. Dissolve cornstarch in remaining water.
Add to apples. Continue to cook, stirring constantly,
until thickened. Remove from heat and add Equal®.
Pour into baked Pie Crust. Chill before serving or serve
warm.

Makes one 8- or 9-inch pie.
Serves 8.
Calories per serving: 221.
Diabetic exchanges per serving: milk 0,
*   vegetable 0, fruit 1, bread 1, meat 0, fat 2.*

Blueberry Pie

8- or 9-inch baked Pie Crust (page 77)

Filling: 4 cups fresh or frozen unsweetened
blueberries, thawed
½ teaspoon lemon rind
½ teaspoon cinnamon
1 tablespoon diet margarine
½ cup water
¼ cup cornstarch
10 packets Equal®
Diet whipped topping (optional)

Prepare Pie Crust and set aside.

In a heavy saucepan, combine blueberries, lemon rind, cinnamon, shortening, and ¼ cup water. Bring to a boil. Cover. Reduce heat and simmer until blueberries are soft. Dissolve cornstarch in remaining water; add to blueberries. Stir until thickened. Continue to cook and stir for 1 extra minute. Remove from heat. Stir in Equal®. Cool. Pour into baked Pie Crust. If desired, top with a dollup of low-calorie whipped topping.

Makes one 8- or 9-inch pie.
Serves 8.
Calories per serving: 216.
Diabetic exchanges per serving: milk 0,
    vegetable 0, fruit 1, bread 1, meat 0, fat 2.

Cherry Pie

8- or 9-inch baked Pie Crust (page 77)

Filling: **3 cups canned, unsweetened, pitted**
            red cherries, drained (reserve juice)
¾ cup cherry juice
¼ cup cornstarch
1 tablespoon diet margarine
2 teaspoons lemon juice
10 packets Equal®
Diet whipped topping (optional)

Prepare Pie Crust and set aside.

In a heavy saucepan, bring cherries and ½ cup cherry juice to a boil. Dissolve cornstarch in remaining juice. Add to cherries. Continue to cook, stirring constantly, until filling thickens. Stir in diet margarine and lemon juice and continue to cook for 1 minute. Remove from heat. Stir in Equal®. Pour into baked Pie Crust. Top with low-calorie whipped topping.

Makes one 8- or 9-inch pie.
Serves 8.
Calories per serving: 275.
Diabetic exchanges per serving: milk 0,
    vegetables 0, fruit 2, bread 1, meat 0, fat 2.

Pumpkin Pie

8- or 9-inch baked Pie Crust (page 77)

Filling: **1½ cups canned pumpkin pie filling**
1½ cups half-and-half
½ teaspoon salt
1 teaspoon cinnamon
½ teaspoon ginger
½ teaspoon nutmeg
3 eggs slightly beaten
1 envelope unflavored gelatin
¼ cup water
8 packets Equal®

Prepare Pie Crust and set aside.
In top of a double boiler, combine pumpkin, half-and-half, salt, spices, and eggs. Cook over hot water until filling thickens. Remove from heat. Soften gelatin in cold water, stirring to dissolve gelatin. Add to pumpkin mixture and stir well. Stir in Equal®. Refrigerate pumpkin filling until it begins to thicken. Pour into prepared Pie Crust. Refrigerate until filling is set.

Makes one 8- or 9-inch pie.
Serves 8.
Calories per serving: 300.
Diabetic exchanges per serving: milk 0,
    vegetable 0, fruit 0, bread 2, meat 0, fat 3.

Easy Pumpkin Pie

8- or 9-inch Graham Cracker Crust
(page 79)

Filling: 1 envelope unflavored gelatin
1 teaspoon ground cinnamon
½ teaspoon ginger
½ teaspoon nutmeg
¼ teaspoon salt
2 eggs
1 can (13 oz.) evaporated skim milk
1 can (16 oz.) pumpkin
8 packets Equal®

Prepare Graham Cracker Crust and set aside.
Mix gelatin, spices, and salt in a medium saucepan.
Beat eggs and milk together and pour into dry ingredients. Let stand 1 minute. Stir over low heat until
gelatin is dissolved, about 10 minutes. Stir in pumpkin
and Equal®. Pour mixture into prepared Graham
Cracker Crust. Chill until firm.

Makes one 8- or 9-inch pie.
Serves 8.
Calories per serving: 92.
Diabetic exchanges per serving: milk 1,
   vegetable 0, fruit 0, bread 0, meat 0, fat 0.

Peach Pie

8- or 9-inch baked Pie Crust (page 77)

Filling: 1 package (20 oz.) frozen, unsweetened peaches, thawed
2 teaspoons lemon juice
3 tablespoons water
2 tablespoons cornstarch
8 packets Equal®
1 cup whipping cream

Prepare Pie Crust and set aside.

Sprinkle peaches with lemon juice; reserve a few slices for garnish. In a blender, puree 1 cup peaches; pour into a heavy saucepan. Bring to a boil, stirring constantly. Dissolve cornstarch in water. Add to pureed peaches. Continue to cook, stirring constantly, until thickened. Remove from heat. Stir in 4 packets of Equal®. Pour filling into Pie Crust. Chill.

Beat whipping cream with remaining 4 packets of Equal®. Spread whipped cream over top of pie and garnish with remaining peach slices. Chill until firm.

> *Makes one 8- or 9-inch pie.*
> *Serves 8.*
> *Calories per serving: 196.*
> *Diabetic exchanges per serving: milk 0,*
>   *vegetable 0, fruit 0, bread 1, meat 0, fat 2.*

Strawberry Pie ♥

9-inch Graham Cracker Crust (page 79)

Filling: **2½ cups fresh strawberries**
           2 envelopes unflavored gelatin
           ¾ cup water
           2 egg whites
           2 packets Equal®
           1 envelope (1¼ oz.) low-calorie dessert topping mix

Prepare Graham Cracker Crust and set aside.

Reserve a few strawberries for garnish. In large mixing bowl, crush enough of the remaining berries to measure 1½ cups. Set aside. In small saucepan, combine gelatin and water; heat and stir till gelatin dissolves. Cool 20 minutes; stir into the crushed strawberrries. Chill to the consistency of corn syrup, stirring occasionally.

Remove from the refrigerator (gelatin mixture will continue to set). Beat egg whites till soft peaks form.

Gradually add Equal®, beating till stiff peaks form.
When gelatin is consistency of unbeaten egg whites,
fold in stiff, beaten egg whites.

Prepare topping mix according to package directions.
Fold into strawberry mixture. Chill till mixture mounds
when spooned. Pile mixture into pie shell; chill 8 hours
or until firm. Garnish with reserved strawberries.

Makes one 9-inch pie.
Serves 8.
Calories per serving: 35.
Diabetic exchanges per serving: milk 0,
    vegetable 0, fruit ½, bread 0, meat 0, fat 0.

Strawberry Chiffon Pie

**8- or 9-inch Graham Cracker Crust
    (page 79)**

Filling: **2 envelopes unflavored gelatin
    ½ cup cold water
    2 egg yolks
    6 packets Equal®
    1 tablespoon lemon juice
    2 cups crushed, unsweetened straw-
        berries, fresh or frozen
    2 egg whites
    ¼ cup evaporated skim milk, chilled
    Whole strawberries (optional for
        garnish)**

Prepare Graham Cracker Crust and set aside.

Soften gelatin in cold water. (If using frozen berries,
defrost and drain the berries and use the drained juice
instead of water.) Beat together egg yolks and Equal®.
Add softened gelatin and cook over low heat, stirring
frequently, until gelatin is dissolved and mixture
thickens slightly.

Remove from heat and add lemon juice. Chill until
mixture mounds when dropped from a spoon; fold in

strawberries. Beat egg whites until stiff peaks form and fold into strawberry mixture. Beat chilled evaporated milk until soft peaks form, then fold it into strawberry mixture. Pour into prepared Graham Cracker Crust.

Garnish with whole strawberries, leaving green stems on.

Makes one 8- or 9-inch pie.
Serves 8.
Calories per serving: 126.
Diabetic exchanges per serving: milk 0,
    vegetable 0, fruit 0, bread 1, meat 0, fat 1.

Quick Strawberry Pie

8- or 9-inch Graham Cracker Crust
(page 79)

Filling: **1 envelope unflavored gelatin**
    ¼ cup cold water
    2 cups plain low-fat yogurt
    2 cups fresh, chopped strawberries
    8 packets Equal®
    1 envelope diet dessert topping

Prepare Graham Cracker Crust and set aside.

In a small saucepan, soften gelatin in cold water. Stir over low heat until gelatin dissolves completely. Stir into yogurt. Mash strawberries and fold them into yogurt. Stir in Equal®. Pour into Graham Cracker Crust. When pie is firm, whip dessert topping and spread on top of pie. Chill.

Makes one 8- or 9-inch pie.
Serves 8.
Calories per serving: 135.
Diabetic exchanges per serving: milk 0,
    vegetable 0, fruit 0, bread 1, meat 0, fat 1.

Pie Crusts

What I remember most about pies for dessert when I was a child is the special treat we would have waiting after school on pie baking day. Not the pie, which was for dessert that evening, but the trimmings. My grandmother would take the trimmings from the pastry and re-roll them, cut, and sprinkle them with sugar and cinnamon for an extra treat. Since she baked a number of pies at a time, that meant plenty of trimmings! You can do this too, and your children will love it.

There's not much to a pie crust—just flour, shortening, a little salt, and water—but the quality of this simple pastry is regarded as the measure of a cook's ability. It has to be good tasting, beautifully and evenly browned, and flaky.

Now more than ever cooks are turning to pie crusts that can be made in minutes and don't require baking. These, like the old fashioned kind, are delicious, and many offer the benefit of being low calorie.

Tips for Successful Pie Crusts

- Handle pastry dough as little as possible; unlike bread dough, pastry dough that's overhandled will become tough. As soon as dough holds together enough to form a ball, flatten the ball and roll the dough out to the size specified.
- Always roll pastry dough from the center to the edge. That way, your crust will be even in size and thickness.
- Turn the dough gently as you roll it to prevent it from sticking.
- For a good size marker, use your pie plate! Turn it upside down on the rolled dough. Then you can judge how much more rolling to do.
- To help center the pastry dough in your pie plate, fold the rolled pastry in half over your rolling pin; lay one half over the pie plate. When the rolling pin is across the center, flip the other half over the rest of the pie plate.
- Be sure to fit the dough loosely in your pie plate. If the dough is stretched taut, it will shrink during baking.
- There's another way to bake your unfilled pastry shell smooth and bubble-free besides pricking all over with a fork. Fit a piece of foil or wax paper in the bottom of the plate over the pastry. Fill the shell with rice or beans (which can be reused); then bake 5 minutes or until pastry is set. Remove rice or beans and foil or wax paper. Continue to bake until crust is golden brown.

Baked Pie Crust

1¼ cups flour
1 teaspoon salt
⅓ cup vegetable oil
2 tablespoons ice water

In a mixing bowl, combine flour and salt. Measure oil and water but do not mix; add to the flour mixture. Stir until well blended. With your hands, form a smooth ball. Place on a sheet of waxed paper and flatten a little. Cover with another sheet of waxed paper, and roll out with a rolling pin to desired size and thickness.

Peel off top paper. Invert dough and with paper on top, place it in pie pan; then carefully peel off paper. Fit dough into pan and press it around edge with fork Prick crust in several places on bottom with fork. Bake 10 to 12 minutes at 450°. Crust should be lightly browned.

Makes one 8- or 9-inch pie crust.
Serves 8.
Calories per serving (8" crust without filling): 150
Diabetic exchanges per serving (8" crust without filling):
milk 0, vegetable 0, fruit 1, bread 0, meat 0, fat 2.

Zwieback Crust

1 cup finely-crushed zwieback
2 tablespoons diet margarine, melted
1 tablespoon honey
1 packet Equal®

Combine zwieback, margarine, honey, and Equal®. Reserve 2 tablespoons of mixture for the topping. Press remaining mixture onto bottom of sprayed (use vegetable spray) 7- or 8-in. spring-form pan. Chill.

Makes one 7- or 8-inch pie crust; or one 7- or 8-inch cheesecake crust.
Serves 8.
Calories per serving (8" crust without filling): 68.
Diabetic exchanges per serving (8" crust without filling):
milk 0, vegetable 0, fruit 1, bread 0, meat 0, fat 0.

Chocolate Crumb Crust

½ cup vanilla wafer crumbs
1 tablespoon unsweetened cocoa
1½ tablespoons diet margarine,
melted
2 packets Equal®

In small bowl, combine crumbs and cocoa; add margarine and stir until evenly blended. Stir Equal® in well. Press mixture evenly on bottom of 9-in. springform pan.

Makes one 9-inch crust.
Serves 8.
Calories per serving (without filling): 40.
Diabetic exchanges per serving (without
filling): milk 0, vegetable 0, fruit 0, bread
½, meat 0, fat 0.

Graham Cracker Crust ♥

1¼ cups graham cracker crumbs
⅓ cup diet margarine, melted

Combine crumbs with melted diet margarine in a bowl. Press firmly on bottom and sides of a 9- or 10-in. pie pan. Bake in preheated 350° oven 8 to 10 minutes. Cool.

Makes one 9- or 10-inch crust.
Serves 8.
Calories per serving (9" crust without filling): 80.
Diabetic exchanges per serving (9" crust without filling):
milk 0, vegetable 0, fruit 0, bread ½, meat 0, fat 1.

Cakes

One of my biggest moments as a child was the first time I baked a cake. My grandmother and I planned it for several days. I will never forget my triumph when I opened the oven and saw the finished cake, dense and chocolate. I carefully removed it from the oven and placed it on the cake rack to cool. Later, with grandmother's help, I removed the cake from the pan and stood there in awe. Since it was lunchtime, we decided to take a break and took our lunch out onto the patio before making the frosting.

Imagine my surprise when we returned to the kitchen and I saw Prince, my dog, licking his chops. He had just taken a huge bite out of my cake after jumping onto a chair. My grandmother, possessing great wisdom, announced that we had no problem. We would simply make chocolate petit fours. After cutting away the dog-bitten edge, we cut the cake into two-inch squares. We prepared the frosting, and, wonder of wonders! who would ever know.

I relate this story because I feel that most cooks panic when something goes wrong, even though mishaps can be corrected. Take the cake with the filling that doesn't set up properly. Just cut the cake up, place it in a dessert dish, and spoon the filling over it. *Voilla!* pudding cake.

The recipes in this chapter truly prove that you can have your cake and eat it too. With a pot of freshly-brewed coffe or tea alongside, these cakes make ideal light snacks or desserts.

Tips for Successful Cakes

- When baking a cake, never use vegetable oil or melted shortening unless the recipe especially calls for it; otherwise, your cake will turn out heavy and tough and may sink in the middle.
- The easiest way to tell if a cake is done is to touch it lightly in the center. If it springs back it is done. Another test is to insert a wooden pick in the center of the cake. If shortening or crumbs cling to the pick, bake the cake for 5 minutes more and test it again.
- Always leave cakes in pans on wire racks for at least 10 minutes to cool. Loosen sides with a knife, invert each cake pan on wire rack or plate, remove pan, and immediately turn cake right-side-up on wire rack to complete cooling.
- To split a cake into layers, measure vertically with a ruler; mark cake all around with wooden picks. Slice across tops of picks, using a long, serrated knife and cutting with a slow motion.

Frosting a Cake:

- Slice off any "bumps" with a sharp knife. Place one layer upside-down on serving plate so flat surface faces up; brush off crumbs.
- Spread frosting on flat surface to the edge.
- Place the flat side of next layer on frosted surface and secure layers with toothpicks to prevent them from moving. Then frost the flat surface of the next layer.
- After frosting the interior surfaces, next do sides, then top, swirling frosting with a knife. Remove toothpicks and smooth frosting.

Choco-Mint Roll

Chocolate Sponge Cake (page 93)

Filling   **⅓ cup nonfat dry milk**
2 tablespoons cornstarch
Dash salt
1 cup water
2 well beaten eggs
8 packets Equal®
Few drops of peppermint extract

In a saucepan, combine the milk powder, cornstarch, and dash of salt. Add 1 cup water. Cook and stir over medium heat till mixture is bubbly; cook and stir 2 minutes more. Remove from heat. Stir about half the hot mixture into the beaten eggs; return all to saucepan. Cook and stir till bubbly; cook and stir 2 minutes more. Remove from heat. Stir in the Equal® and peppermint extract. Cover with clear plastic wrap; cool for about 2 hours. Unroll cake; spread with filling; roll up. Cover and chill. Slice to serve.

Serves 10.
Calories per serving: 120.
Diabetic exchanges per serving: milk 0,
   vegetable 0, fruit 0, bread 1, meat 0, fat 1.

Cheeseless Cheesecake

1 cup crushed pineapple, with juice
⅔ cup nonfat dry milk
1 packet unflavored gelatin
2 packets Equal®
½ tablespoon vanilla extract
½ tablespoon lemon juice
½ teaspoon butter flavoring
¼ cup boiling water
Cinnamon to taste

Drain pineapple and set aside. Mix gelatin into pineapple; stir well. Add boiling water and some of drained juice. Put into blender and blend for 1 minute. Add remaining juice and other ingredients. Blend at high speed until frothy. Pour into pie plate. Sprinkle with ground cinnnamon and chill at least 2 hours.

Serves 2.
Calories per serving: 120.
Diabetic exchanges per serving: milk ½,
*   vegetable 0, fruit 1, bread 0, meat 0, fat 0.*

Cappuccino Angel Cake with Coffee Sauce

Cake: **1 angel food cake (purchased or**
       home-baked)
       ¼ to ⅓ cup crème de cacao
       1 envelope diet dessert topping mix
       2 tablespoons cocoa
       2 packets Equal®
       2 tablespoons sliced, toasted almonds
       or chopped nuts

Sauce: **½ cup cocoa**
        ½ strong coffee
        4 packets Equal®
        ¼ cup skim milk

To Make Cake: Place cake, bottom up, on serving plate. With cake tester or fork, poke holes in bottom and spoon on liqueur, letting it seep into cake. Whip topping mix according to package directions. Add cream, cocoa, and 2 packets Equal®. Use to frost cake lightly. Sprinkle with nuts. Chill 1 to 2 hours. Just before serving, drizzle coffee sauce over frosting. Pass remainder of sauce when serving cake.

To Make Coffee Sauce: In small saucepan, combine cocoa, coffee, and skim milk. Cook and stir over medium heat until slightly thickened and smooth. Remove from heat and add Equal®. Cool. Makes 1 cup.

> *Serves 8.*
> *Calories per serving: 200.*
> *Diabetic exchanges per serving: milk 0,*
> *vegetable 0, fruit 0, bread 2, meat 0, fat 1.*

A luscious party dessert. Everyone just loves it!

Grand Marnier Cake

> 1 angel food cake
> 1 can (6 oz.) frozen orange juice, melted
> 1 jar (8 to 10 oz.) fruit-only orange marmalade
> 1 jigger Grand Marnier
> 1 envelope diet dessert topping mix
> 3 packets Equal®
> 1 teaspoon Grand Marnier
> Toasted, slivered almonds

Cool orange juice and combine with orange marmalade mixtue. Poke holes in cake from top to bottom, using cake tester or fork. Do not break the side walls. Drizzle the orange mixture slowly into the holes until all is used. Refrigerate 24 hours or freeze at this time. A few hours before serving, sprinkle one jigger of Grand Marnier over cake. Then ice with topping mix, whipped with 3 packets of Equal® and 1 teaspoon Grand Marnier added.

Sprinkle toasted, slivered almonds on top.

> *Serves 12.*
> *Calories per serving: 200.*
> *Diabetic exchanges per serving: milk 0,*
> *vegetable 0, fruit 2, bread 1, meat 0, fat 0.*

Snowflake Cake

1½ envelopes unflavored gelatin
6 tablespoons cold water
1 cup orange juice with pulp
Juice of 1 lemon
10 packets Equal®
1 purchased or home-made angel
  food cake
2 envelopes diet dessert topping mix
¼ cup unsweetened, grated coconut

Dissolve gelatin in cold water. Stir orange juice, lemon juice, and Equal® until dissolved; add to gelatin. Refrigerate until mixture just starts to set, about 15 minutes. Whip ½ topping mix and fold into gelatin mixture. Line bottom of round bowl with waxed paper. Put in a layer of gelatin mixture, then pieces of angel food cake (from which brown crusts have been removed), then another layer of gelatin. Repeat. Pack in solid; chill overnight. Unmold onto serving dish. Whip remaining diet dessert topping according to package directions and frost. Sprinkle with coconut.

Serves 12.
Calories per serving: 166.
Diabetic exchanges per serving: milk 0,
    vegetable 0, fruit 0, bread 2, meat 0, fat 0.

Peaches 'n Cream Angel Cake

1 purchased or home-made angel
  food cake
1 package (3 oz.) cream cheese,
  softened
7 ounces of Eagle brand sweetened
  condensed milk (not evaporated
  milk)
⅓ cup lemon juice

1 teaspoon almond extract
2 to 3 drops yellow food coloring
   (optional)
1 envelope diet dessert topping mix,
   whipped with 2 packets Equal®
1 cup chopped, fresh peeled peaches
2 packets Equal®
Additional fresh peach slices for
   garnish

Cut 1-in. slice crosswise from top of cake; set aside. With sharp knife, cut around cake 1 in. from center hole and 1 in. from outer edge, leaving bottom 1" of cake intact to serve as base. Remove center portion of cake and tear it into bite-sized pieces; reserve.

In larger mixer bowl, beat cheese until fluffy. Gradually beat in sweetened condensed milk until smooth. Stir in lemon juice, almond extract, and, if desired, food coloring. Fold in ⅓ of topping mix; reserve ⅔ for topping. Refrigerate.

Place cut peaches in a bowl and sprinkle with Equal®. Fold peaches and reserved, torn cake pieces into remaining cream mixture; fill cake cavity. Replace top slice of cake; frost with reserved topping mix. Chill 3 hours or until set. Garnish with additional peaches if desired. Store in refrigerator.

Makes one 10-inch cake.
Serves 10.
Calories per serving (without cream cheese):
   323.
Diabetic exchanges per serving (without cream
   cheese): milk 0, vegetables 0, fruit 0,
   bread 0, meat 0, fat 0.

Calories per serving (complete recipe): 350.
Diabetic exchanges per serving (complete rec-
   ipe): milk 1, vegetable 0, fruit 3½, bread 0,
   meat 0, fat 1.

Classic Carrot Cake with Topping

Cake:
- 2 cups flour
- 2 teaspoons baking soda
- 2 teaspoons cinnamon
- ½ teaspoon ginger
- ½ teaspoon salt
- 3 eggs
- ¾ cup diet mayonnaise
- 2 cups grated carrots
- 1 can (18 oz.) unsweetened crushed pineapple, undrained
- 1 teaspoon vanilla
- ½ cup chopped walnuts

Topping:
- 1 envelope diet dessert topping mix
- 1 teaspoon vanilla
- 8 packets Equal®

To Make Cake: In a large mixing bowl, combine flour, baking soda, cinnamon, ginger, and salt. In another bowl, beat together eggs and mayonnaise. Gradually beat in flour mixture. Stir in the remaining ingredients. Pour into a greased and lightly-floured 8-in. square pan. Bake at 350° for 30 to 35 minutes or until a toothpick inserted in the center comes out clean. Cool in pan for 10 minutes. Remove from pan. Cool completely.

To Make Topping: Prepare topping according to directions on package. Beat in vanilla and Equal®. Spread over cake.

Makes one 8-inch cake.
Serves 8.
Calories per serving: 220.
Diabetic exchanges per serving: milk 0,
   vegetable 0, fruit ½, bread 2, meat 0, fat 1.

Delicious Apple Cake with Topping

Cake: 1½ cups flour
         2 teaspoons baking soda
         ½ teaspoon salt
         1 teaspoon cinnamon
         1 teaspoon nutmeg
         ½ cup diet margarine, softened
         2 eggs
         ¼ cup water
         ¼ cup frozen apple juice concentrate,
           thawed
         4 cups peeled, chopped Delicious
           apples
         1 cup Post Grape-Nuts
         ½ cup raisins

Topping: 1 envelope diet dessert topping mix
         4 packets Equal®
         1 teaspoon vanilla

To Make Cake: In a large mixing bowl, combine flour,
baking soda, salt, cinnamon, and nutmeg. In another
bowl, cream together shortening and eggs. Beat in flour
mixture. Stir in water and apple juice. Fold in apples,
Post Grape-Nuts, and raisins. Pour into a greased and
lightly-floured 8-inch square pan. Bake for 30 to 35
minutes or until a toothpick inserted in the center
comes out clean. Cool cake. Remove from pan.
To Make Topping: Beat topping mix according to directions on package until thick peaks form. Beat in Equal®
and vanilla. Spread over cake. Refrigerate any leftovers.

Makes one 8-inch-square cake.
Serves 8.
Calories per serving: 272.
Diabetic exchanges per serving: milk 0,
  vegetable 0, fruit 1, bread 2, meat 0, fat 1.

Banana Nut Cake with Banana Cream Frosting

Cake: **2 cups all-purpose flour**
1 tablespoon baking powder
½ teaspoon salt
¼ cup vegetable oil
2 eggs
½ cup skimmed milk
1 teaspoon vanilla
1 cup mashed ripe bananas
½ cup chopped walnuts

Frosting: **1 package (8 oz.) low-calorie cream cheese**
½ cup banana yogurt
10 packets Equal®
1 teaspoon vanilla

To Make Cake: Sift together dry ingredients. Blend oil, eggs, skim milk, and vanilla until smooth. Stir in bananas. Add to dry ingredients and stir just until flour is thoroughly moistened. Add walnuts, reserving a few for garnish. Pour equal amounts of batter into two 8-in. round cake pans sprayed with non-stick coating. Bake in preheated 350° oven 20 minutes or until toothpick inserted in center comes out clean. Remove from pans; cool completely on wire racks. Frost cake with Banana Cream frosting.

To Make Frosting: Combine cream cheese and yogurt; blend until smooth. Stir in remaining ingredients. Chill before using. Spread frosting over each layer.

Makes one double-layer, 9-inch cake.
Serves 12.
Calories per serving: 166.
Diabetic exchanges per serving: milk 0,
    vegetable 0, fruit 0, bread 1, meat 0, fat 1½.

Strawberry Cake Roll

Cake: 5 eggs, separated
          2 tablespoons water
          1 tablespoon vanilla
          ¾ cup all-purpose flour
          1 teaspoon baking powder
          6 packets Equal®

Filling: 1 packet low-calorie whipped topping
             mix
          ½ cup skim milk
          4 ounces low-calorie cream cheese,
             softened
          4 packets Equal®
          1 cup chopped strawberries
          Whole strawberries and mint sprigs
             (optional garnish)

To Make Cake: Beat egg yolks and water until thick and lemon-colored. Gradually fold in flour and baking powder. Beat egg whites until stiff, but not dry, and peaks form. Beat in egg yolk mixture. Spread batter onto wax-paper-lined 11×15-in. jelly roll pan sprayed with non-stick coating. Bake in preheated 400° oven 10 to 12 minutes. Remove from pan immediately and place on clean kitchen towel. Remove wax paper and sprinkle 6 packets of Equal® over cake. Roll cake up, jelly roll fashion, starting with shorter side. Cool cake, then unroll. Prepare filling as directed.

To Make Filling: Prepare whipped topping mix according to package directions, using skim milk instead of water. Beat topping with cream cheese and Equal® until smooth. Fold in strawberries. Spread mixture over unrolled cake, leaving a ½ in. to 1-in. margin around edges. Roll up cake with filling and refrigerate until ready to serve. Slice with serrated knife.

Garnish with whole strawberries and mint sprigs.

Makes one 10-inch roll, or 10 servings.
Calories per serving: 95.
Diabetic exchanges per serving: milk 0,
    vegetable 0, fruit ½, bread 0, meat 1, fat 0.

Skinny Strawberry Shortcake

½ cup whole-wheat pastry flour
½ cup unbleached white flour
1 teaspoon baking powder
3 tablespoons chilled margarine
6 to 8 tablespoons skim milk, divided
4 cups sliced strawberries
6 packets Equal®
1 envelope diet dessert topping mix,
  whipped

To Make Shortcakes: Preheat oven to 425°. Spray a baking sheet with vegetable spray. In a medium-size bowl, whisk together whole-wheat pastry flour, unbleached white flour, and baking powder. Cut in margarine with a pastry blender until mixture is crumbly. With a wooden spoon, stir in ¼ cup (4 tablespoons) of the skim milk. Add more milk, 1 tablespoon at a time, until dough clings together. Divide dough into 6 pieces and drop onto prepared baking sheet. Bake on middle shelf of oven for 10 minutes. Remove to wire racks to cool.

To Assemble: Split shortcakes in half. Sprinkle Equal® on strawberries and mix well. Layer the strawberries and dessert topping over the shortcakes, finishing with topping mix.
This recipe can be used to make any fruit shortcake, such as blueberry or peach.

Serves 6.
Calories per serving: 140.
Diabetic exchanges per serving: milk 0,
  vegetable 0, fruit 1, bread 1, meat 0, fat 0.

Chocolate Sponge Cake

¾ cup sifted all-purpose flour
1 teaspoon baking powder
5 eggs, separated
⅛ teaspoon salt
½ cup brewed coffee
⅓ cup unsweetened cocoa
10 packets Equal®

Spray bottom of a 15½ × 10½ × 1-in. jelly-roll pan with vegetable spray. Line bottom with waxed paper. Spray again with vegetable spray. Preheat oven to 400°. Sift together flour and baking powder onto a piece of waxed paper. Reserve.

In a large bowl, at high speed, beat egg whites with salt until stiff peaks form. Beat egg yolks with coffee and cocoa till well blended. Beat in reserved flour mixture. Gently fold in beaten egg whites until no white streaks remain.

Turn batter into prepared jelly-roll pan and bake 5 to 7 minutes. Test cake by tapping center with your fingertip; cake should spring back if done. Remove from oven and loosen cake around edges with knife. Invert onto a clean towel, and peel off waxed paper. Sprinkle cake with 10 packets of Equal®.

Starting with short end, roll up cake and towel together. Place roll, seam side down, on rack. Cool. Prepare filling or sauce of your choice such as Classic Light Fruit Sauce or Vanilla Rum Sauce (see Index).

Serves 10.
Calories per serving: 87.
Diabetic exchanges per serving: milk 0,
 vegetable 0, fruit 0, bread ½, meat ½, fat 0.

Puddings, Mousses, Soufflés, and Gelatins

There are those of us who still cling to the comforting memory of certain desserts whose soothing tastes and textures always remind us of home. Puddings are excellent for the calorie watcher. They can be made with luscious fruits, slimming gelatin, frothy egg whites, whipped milk, and other delightful ingredients that don't add many calories.

Mousses and soufflés have always spelled sophistication. Their elegant appearance make them impressive desserts, yet they are easily prepared and require a minimal amount of last-minute work.

Tips for Successful Puddings, Mousses, Soufflés, and Gelatins

- How to Separate Eggs:
  1. To separate an egg, first set out two small bowls. Holding the egg in one hand, tap it sharply in the middle with a knife or tap it on the edge of one of the bowls.
  2. Hold the egg over one bowl; pull the shell apart, tilting it so that the yolk remains in one half of the shell.
  3. Pour yolk back and forth from one half of the shell to the other until all white runs into one bowl. Drop the yolk into the second bowl.
- To preserve the flavor of flavorings, add them after removing your mixture from the stove.
- Cover your finished puddings with plastic wrap to prevent a skin from forming.
- Egg whites will not whip well in the presence of fat, so make sure your bowl and beaters are perfectly clean. If there is a particle of egg yolk or other matter in the whites, spoon it out.
- Well-beaten whites stand up in glossy peaks. Do not overbeat egg whites or they will become dry. Dry egg whites will clump when folded into sauces or other mixtures.

Pineapple Air

1 can (8 oz.) crushed pineapple (juice packed)
3 tablespoons nonfat dry milk
2 beaten egg yolks
1 packet Equal®
½ teaspoon vanilla
2 egg whites
1 packet Equal®
4 pineapple chunks (optional for garnish)

Drain pineapple well, reserving juice. Chill pineapple. Add water to reserved juice, if necessary, to make ½ cup. Dissolve dry milk powder in pineapple juice.

In a small, heavy saucepan, combine the milk mixture and egg yolks. Cook over low heat, stirring constantly till mixture thickens and coats a metal spoon. Remove from heat and stir in 1 packet of Equal®. Place saucepan in a pan of ice water to cool. Stir in vanilla. When cooled, cover and chill the egg mixture for 2 to 4 hours.

At serving time, fold pineapple into cooked mixture. Using an electric mixer and small mixer bowl, beat egg whites at high speed till soft peaks form. Gradually add 1 packet Equal®, beating till stiff peaks form. Gently fold egg whites into the pineapple mixture. Spoon into chilled serving dishes.

Garnish with pineapple chunk.

Makes 4 servings.
Calories per serving: 97.
Diabetic exchanges per serving: milk 0,
vegetable 0, fruit 1, bread 0, meat 0, fat ½.

Miniature Strawberry Charlottes

1 recipe Rum Custard Sauce (page 36)
6 ladyfingers, halved
1 cup strawberries, sliced (reserve 2 whole)
3 packets Equal®
1 envelope diet dessert topping mix, whipped

To assemble: Line bottom and sides of 2 large balloon wine glasses or 2 bowls with ladyfingers, rounded sides out. Spoon some of the custard into each. Sprinkle strawberries with Equal®, and top custard with several strawberry slices. Cover with some whipped topping. Continue layering with remaining ingredients, ending with whipped topping.

> *Makes 2 servings.*
> *Calories per serving: 186.*
> *Diabetic exchanges per serving: milk 0,*
>   *vegetable 0, fruit 0, bread 1, meat 0, fat 2.*

Strawberry Cloud

> **¼ cup cold water**
> **¾ cup apple juice**
> **1 envelope unflavored gelatin**
> **½ cup plain low-fat yogurt**
> **1 egg**
> **1 cup fresh or frozen unsweetened**
>   **strawberries**
> **1 packet of Equal®**

If using frozen strawberries, thaw at room temperature, drain, and set aside. If using fresh strawberries, wash, drain, hull, and set aside. Combine the water and apple juice in a small saucepan; sprinkle with gelatin and let rest for 2 minutes. Heat over low heat until gelatin has dissolved, stirring constantly. Remove from heat and allow to cool until the mixture starts to thicken.

Combine the yogurt, egg, strawberries, and Equal® in a blender or food processor and puree until smooth. Add the apple juice mixture and blend. Pour into 4 dessert dishes and refrigerate 4–5 hours.

> *Makes 4 servings.*
> *Calories per serving: 70.*
> *Diabetic exchanges per serving: milk 1,*
>   *vegetable 0, fruit 0, bread 0, meat 0, fat 0.*

Strawberry Mousse

¼ cup fresh orange juice
1 envelope unflavored gelatin
1 egg
1 egg yolk
1 cup fresh strawberries, hulled
1 tablespoon dark rum
⅓ cup whipping cream, whipped to
   soft peaks
6 packets Equal®
Few drops of red food coloring
Sliced strawberries for garnish

Oil a 3-cup mold (or two 1-cup soufflé dishes fitted with foil collars). Place orange juice in cup. Sprinkle with gelatin and let stand until liquid is absorbed, about 5 minutes. Meanwhile, combine whole egg and yolk in medium bowl of electric mixer and beat at high speed until mixture is thick when beaters are lifted, about 5 to 7 minutes. Set aside.

Combine strawberries and rum in processor or blender and puree until smooth. Set cup with gelatin mixture in small pan of hot water and place over low heat until gelatin is completely dissolved and clear. Stir into egg mixture. Blend in the pureed strawberries.

Set bowl in larger bowl of ice water and stir gently with rubber spatula until mixture is almost set, about 10 minutes. Fold in whipped cream and Equal®. Stir again with spatula to mix well. Mix in food coloring and pour into prepared dish(es). Refrigerate until set.

If using mold, invert onto platter before serving. If using soufflé dishes, remove collars just before serving to show off the mousse above edges of dishes. Garnish top with berry slices.

Makes 2 servings.
Calories per serving: 150.
Diabetic exchanges per serving: milk 0,
   vegetable 0, fruit 1, bread 0, meat 1, fat 0.

Orange Mousse ♥

> ⅔ cup hot water
> 2 envelopes unflavored gelatin
> 2 packets Equal®
> 1 can (6 oz.) unsweetened orange
>   juice concentrate, partially thawed
> 2 tablespoons evaporated skim milk
> ½ teaspoon vanilla extract
> 6 to 8 ice cubes
> Orange slices (optional for garnish)

Pour hot water and gelatin into blender. Blend 30 seconds at low setting. Add Equal® and continue blending 10 seconds longer. Add orange juice concentrate, evaporated skim milk, and vanilla. Set blender on high setting, add ice cubes gradually, and blend until ice is dissolved. Pour into parfait glasses and chill. Garnish with a slice of orange.

Makes 6 servings.
Calories per serving: 50.
Diabetic exchanges per serving: milk 0,
*   vegetable 0, fruit 1, bread 0, meat 0, fat 0.*

Rice Pudding ♥

> 2 cups water
> ½ cup white rice, uncooked
> ¼ cup raisins
> 2 tablespoons cornstarch
> 1¼ cups skim milk
> 1 teaspoon vanilla extract
> 6 packets Equal®
> Dash of cinnamon

Bring water to a boil in a medium saucepan. Stir in rice and raisins. Return to a boil, then reduce heat to low. Cover and cook 30 minutes.

Mix cornstarch with milk, stirring well. Add to rice mixture, slowly, mixing well. Continue cooking and stirring over low heat until mixture thickens. Remove from heat, add vanilla and Equal®. Stir, and add a dash of cinnamon. Pour into a glass bowl. Garnish with a little cinnamon before serving.

Makes 6 servings.
Calories per serving: 106.
Diabetic exchanges per serving: milk 0,
   vegetable 0, fruit ½, bread 1, meat 0, fat 0.

Vanilla Pudding ♥

2¾ cups skim milk
¼ cup cornstarch
2 tablespoons diet margarine
1 teaspoon vanilla
8 packets Equal®

In a heavy saucepan, slowly add milk to cornstarch, stirring until dissolved. Cook over medium heat, stirring constantly, until mixture boils. Boil for 1 minute. Remove from heat. Stir in margarine and vanilla. Stir in Equal®. If needed, beat until smooth. Cover and chill thoroughly.

Makes 4 servings.
Calories per serving: 121.
Diabetic exchanges per serving: milk 1,
   vegetable 0, fruit 0, bread 0, meat 0, fat ½.

Strawberry Cheese Parfait

¾ cup 1% low-fat cottage cheese
1 packet Equal®
½ teaspoon almond extract
¼ teaspoon ground cinnamon
1 cup sliced fresh strawberries, divided
2 tablespoons commercial granola
2 whole fresh strawberries

Combine first 4 ingredients in container of an electric blender; cover and process until smooth. Place ¼ cup strawberries into a tall, narrow glass. Top with 3 tablespoons cheese mixture, ¼ cup strawberries, 2 tablespoons cheese mixture, and 1 tablespoon granola. Repeat procedure with remaining ingredients.
Garnish each with a strawberry.

Makes 2 servings.
Calories per serving: 151.
Diabetic exchanges per serving: milk 0,
    vegetable 0, fruit 0, bread 1, meat 1, fat 0.

Cantaloupe Mousse

2 cups cubed cantaloupe
2 tablespoons orange liqueur
2 envelopes unflavored gelatin
¼ cup water
⅓ cup frozen whipped dessert top-
    ping, thawed
Melon slices (optional for garnish)

Place cubed melon and liqueur in a blender container or food processor bowl. Cover and blend or process till smooth.

In a medium saucepan, stir together gelatin and water. Let stand 5 minutes. Cook and stir over low heat till gelatin is dissolved. Stir in pureed cantaloupe mixture.

Chill to the consistency of corn syrup, stirring several times. When gelatin is partially set (consistency of unbeaten egg whites), fold in the dessert topping. Pour into 4 individual ½-cup molds. Chill about 2 hours or until firm.

To serve, unmold onto serving plates. Garnish with fresh melon slices.

Makes 4 servings.
Calories per serving: 83.
Diabetic exchanges per serving: milk 0,
    vegetable 0, fruit 1, bread 0, meat 0, fat ½.

Pineapple-Pear Mold

2 envelopes unflavored gelatin
2½ cups orange juice
1 can (20 oz.) crushed pineapple
  (juice packed)
2 medium pears, peeled, cored, and
  chopped
6 packets Equal®

In a small saucepan, soften gelatin in ½ cup of the orange juice. Stir in undrained crushed pineapple and remaining orange juice. Chill till partially set. Fold in pears and Equal® and turn mixture into a 6-cup mold. Chill till firm. Unmold onto a plate.

Makes 8 servings.
Calories per serving: 111.
Diabetic exchanges per serving: milk 0,
  vegetable 0, fruit 2, bread 0, meat 0, fat 0.

Peach Mousse

2 envelopes unflavored gelatin
1 cup frozen unsweetened peach
  slices, thawed
1 carton (8 oz.) peach low-fat yogurt
2 packets Equal®
2 egg whites
2 packets Equal®
½ cup whipping cream

In a small saucepan, combine gelatin and ½ cup cold water. Cook and stir over medium heat until gelatin is dissolved. Remove from heat.

In a blender container or food processor bowl, place peach slices. Cover and blend or process till peaches are nearly smooth. Stir peach puree into gelatin mixture. Gradually stir gelatin mixture into yogurt till combined. Add 2 packets Equal®. Chill about 40 minutes or until mixture is the consistency of corn syrup, stirring occasionally. Remove from refrigerator.

In a small mixing bowl, immediately beat egg whites till soft peaks form (tips curl over). Gradually add 2 packets Equal®, beating till stiff peaks form (tips stand straight). Whip the cream till soft peaks form.

When the gelatin mixture is partially set (consistency of unbeaten egg whites), fold in beaten egg whites and whipped cream. Chill about 20 minutes or till mixture mounds when spooned. Pile mixture into 8 dessert dishes and chill in the refrigerator 6 hours or until firm.

Makes 8 servings.
Calories per serving: 50.
Diabetic exchanges per serving: milk ½,
    vegetable 0, fruit 0, bread 0, meat 0, fat 0.

Mocha Bavarian

4 to 5 ladyfingers
¼ cup unsweetened cocoa
1 envelope unflavored gelatin
1 cup skim milk
1 container coffee-flavored low-fat
    yogurt
1 teaspoon instant coffee crystals
⅛ teaspoon mocha extract
6 packets Equal®, divided
⅛ teaspoon cream of tartar
2 egg whites
Fresh grated coconut for garnish
    (optional)

Halve ladyfingers lengthwise, then halve each cross-wise. Around sides of 8-in. spring-form pan, stand up ladyfingers, rounded end up.

In medium-size saucepan, stir together cocoa and gelatin. Add milk; allow to set 1 minute. Over medium heat, bring mixture to a boil, stirring constantly until gelatin is dissolved. Remove from heat; cool about 20 minutes

In large bowl, stir yogurt, coffee crystals, and mocha extract till smooth. Blend in cooled chocolate mixture. Whisk in 4 packets Equal®. Refrigerate about 20 minutes, stirring occasionally.

In small bowl with electric mixer at high speed, beat egg whites and 2 packets Equal® with cream of tartar until stiff peaks form; blend into chocolate mixture. Pour into prepared pan. Cover and chill until set, at least 4 hours. To serve, remove sides of pan and garnish with grated coconut.

Makes one 8-inch cake.
Serves 10.
Calories per serving: 125.
Diabetic exchanges per serving: milk 1,
   vegetable 0, fruit 0, bread 0, meat 0, fat ½.

Peach Crème Fraiche

2 medium-size peaches, sliced
1 cup plain low-fat yogurt
Few drops almond extract
2 packets Equal®
1 envelope unflavored gelatin
2 tablespoons water
Peach slices for garnish

In container of blender, combine peaches, yogurt, and almond extract. Blend until smooth. Add Equal®. In small saucepan, combine gelatin and water until well mixed; place over low heat and stir until gelatin is dissolved. Remove from heat and add to mixture in blender; whip 10 seconds to blend. Chill until mixture begins to thicken. Spoon into champagne flutes and chill. Garnish with peach slices.

Makes 4 servings.
Calories per serving: 63.
Diabetic exchanges per serving: milk 0,
   vegetable 0, fruit 1, bread 0, meat 0, fat 0.

Orange Chiffonade

> 1 envelope unflavored gelatin
> Dash salt
> 1 cup orange juice
> ¼ cup water
> 3 beaten egg yolks
> 2 packets Equal®
> 1 can (11 oz.) mandarin orange sections
> 3 egg whites
> 1 packet Equal®
> ½ of a 4-oz. container of frozen
>   whipped dessert topping, thawed

In a saucepan, combine unflavored gelatin and salt with orange juice and water. Stir in beaten egg yolks. Cook and stir over medium heat 10 to 12 minutes or till slightly thickened and bubbly. Remove from heat and stir in 2 packets of Equal®. Chill, stirring occasionally, just till mixture mounds slightly when spooned.

Drain mandarin orange sections; reserve 8 sections for garnish. Chop up remaining orange sections; fold into gelatin mixture. Beat egg whites with 1 packet Equal® till stiff peaks form; fold into gelatin mixture. Turn mixture into eight 6-oz. custard cups. Cover and chill till firm. Top each with about 1 tablespoon of dessert topping and 1 mandarin orange section.

> *Makes 8 servings.*
> *Calories per serving: 90.*
> *Diabetic exchanges per serving: milk 0,*
>   *vegetable 0, fruit 1, bread 0, meat 0, fat 1.*

Black Bottom Parfait

> 3 squares (3 oz.) unsweetened baking
>   chocolate
> ⅓ cup water
> 10 packets Equal®
> ⅛ teaspoon salt

**1 can (13 oz.) evaporated skim milk,
chilled
1 teaspoon vanilla
2 egg yolks**

Melt chocolate and water in top of double boiler, stirring constantly. Remove from heat and stir in Equal® and salt. Set chocolate aside to cool.

In a large bowl with mixer at high speed, beat milk and vanilla until stiff peaks form. Stir egg yolks into chocolate mixture. Fold chocolate mixture into whipped milk until well mixed. Pour into 8-oz. clear parfait glasses and freeze until firm, at least 4 hours. When frozen, this dessert separates into two layers.

Garnish with diet whipped topping.

> *Makes 8 servings.*
> *Calories per serving: 112.*
> *Diabetic exchanges per serving: milk ½,*
> *   vegetable 0, fruit 0, bread 0, meat 0, fat 1½.*

Jiffy Mocha Mousse (Microwave)

**½ cup semi-sweet chocolate chips
2 tablespoons water
1½ teaspoons instant coffee crystals
2 slightly beaten egg yolks
½ teaspoon vanilla
2 egg whites
⅛ teaspoon cream of tartar
2 packets Equal®
½ cup whipping cream
2 packets Equal®**

In a 2-cup measure, combine chocolate, water, and coffee crystals. Cook in microwave, uncovered, on high (100% power) for 1 to 2 minutes or until mixture is hot and chocolate is soft enough to stir smooth; stir once. Gradually stir hot mixture into egg yolks. Stir in vanilla. Beat with a rotary beater 1 minute. Cool about 5 minutes, stirring occasionally.

Meanwhile, in a small mixer bowl, combine egg whites and cream of tartar. Beat until soft peaks form. Gradually add two packets of Equal®, and continue beating until stiff peaks form. Fold about ⅓ of egg whites into cooled chocolate mixture. Fold mixture into remaining whites.

Beat whipping cream and 2 packets of Equal® until soft peaks form. Fold into mixture. Spoon into 4 dessert dishes. Cover. Chill about 3 hours or until firm. At serving time, top with additional whipped cream if desired.

Makes 4 servings.
Calories per serving: 150.
Diabetic exchanges per serving: milk 0,
    vegetable 0, fruit ½, bread 0, meat 1, fat 1.

This mousse is also an excellent pie filling.

Chocolate Mousse

1 envelope unflavored gelatin
2 cups skim milk
6 tablespoons semi-sweet chocolate
    chips
1 tablespoon cornstarch
1 egg, separated
3 packets Equal®
1 teaspoon vanilla
Dash of salt

In medium saucepan, combine gelatin and milk. Let stand 1 minutes, then add chocolate chips, cornstarch, and egg yolk. Cook over medium heat, stirring constantly, until mixture comes to a full boil. Reduce heat and cook 1 minute longer.

Chill until slightly thickened, stirring occasionally. Set saucepan in a larger bowl of ice cubes. Add Equal® and vanilla. Beat with mixer at high speed, 5 to 6 minutes.

In another bowl, using clean beaters, beat egg white with salt until stiff peaks form. Fold into chocolate mixture. Spoon into 6 individual serving glasses. Chill at least 2 hours before serving.

> *Makes 6 servings.*
> *Calories per serving: 105.*
> *Diabetic exchanges per serving: milk ½,*
> *   vegetable 0, fruit 0, bread 0, meat 0, fat 1.*

White Chocolate Parfait

1 envelope unflavored gelatin
¼ cup cold water
2 cups skim milk, scalded
2 large eggs, separated, at room
**   temperature**
6 packets Equal®
Pinch of salt
1 teaspoon vanilla
½ cup heavy whipping cream, chilled
**   and whipped**
½ cup grated white chocolate
Fresh raspberries (optional for
**   garnish)**

In small bowl, soften gelatin in cold water. Slowly whisk scalded milk into gelatin. In separate bowl, lightly beat egg yolks with Equal® and salt. Slowly add scalded milk mixture, and whisk until Equal® is dissolved.

Set bowl in larger bowl of ice. Stir occasionally until mixture begins to thicken but is not set, about 25 minutes. Stir in vanilla. Beat egg whites until stiff but not dry. Fold into custard. Fold in whipped cream and grated white chocolate.

Spoon into parfait glasses and refrigerate covered for at least 4 hours. Garnish with grated white chocolate and raspberries if desired.

> *Makes 5 servings.*
> *Calories per serving: 158.*
> *Diabetic exchanges per serving: milk 0,*
> *   vegetable 0, fruit ½, bread 0, meat 1, fat 1.*

French Crème with Blackberries

1 carton (8 oz.) low-calorie sour cream
1 cup whipping cream
2 envelopes unflavored gelatin
¼ cup boiling water
1 package (8 oz.) low-calorie cream
  cheese, softened
½ teaspoon vanilla extract
5 packets Equal®
1 cup fresh blackberries
1 packet Equal®

Combine sour cream and whipping cream in a medium saucepan; beat at medium speed with an electric mixer until blended. Cook over low heat until warm. Dissolve gelatin in boiling water. Add to cream mixture; remove from heat.

Beat cream cheese with an electric mixer until light and fluffy. Add cream mixture and vanilla, beating until smooth. Stir in 5 packets of Equal® and blend well. Pour into a lightly-oiled, 4-cup mold; chill until firm. Unmold on a serving platter.

Placing blackberries in a small bowl, sprinkle them with Equal®, and distribute them around the mold.

Makes 8 servings.
Calories per serving: 155.
Diabetic exchanges per serving: milk 0,
   vegetable 0, fruit ½, bread 0, meat 1, fat 1.

Cran-Raspberry Mousse

1 package (10 oz.) frozen raspberries,
  thawed, undrained
1½ cups cranberries
½ cup diet pancake syrup
3 egg whites
⅛ teaspoon cream of tartar

Pinch of salt
8 packets Equal®
¾ cup whipped diet dessert topping
  mix
½ cup cranberries
2 packets Equal®
1 tablespoon diet pancake syrup

Puree raspberries with liquid in processor or blender until smooth, about 1 minute. Press through fine sieve. Set aside.

Combine 1½ cups cranberries and ½ cup syrup in heavy 1-quart, non-aluminum saucepan. Bring to boil over medium-high heat. Reduce heat to medium and cook until cranberries are just tender, stirring mixture occasionally, about 5 minutes. Puree cranberry mixture in processor or blender until smooth, 1 minute. Transfer to large bowl. Refrigerate until chilled.

Using electric mixer, beat whites till foamy, 20 to 30 seconds. Add cream of tartar and salt and beat until soft peaks form, about 1 minute. Beat in 8 packets of Equal®, 1 packet at a time. Continue beating until mixture is thick and glossy.

Stir 3 tablespoons raspberry puree into cranberry mixture. Gently fold whipped topping into cranberry mixture; then fold in whites. Divide mousse mixture among goblets. Cover tightly and freeze until firm.

Mince cranberries with Equal® in processor or blender about 30 seconds. Add remaining raspberry puree and syrup. Blend until smooth, about 1 minute. Refrigerate sauce until well chilled. Let mousse soften in refrigerator 30 minutes. Just before serving, drizzle some of the sauce over each. Pass remaining sauce separately.

Makes 6 servings.
Calories per serving: 105.
Diabetic exchanges per serving: milk 0,
   vegetable 0, fruit ½, bread 1, meat 0, fat 0.

Lemon Mousse

¼ cup + 2 tablespoons lemon juice
1 envelope unflavored gelatin
4 large eggs, separated
2 packets Equal®
1 tablespoon grated lemon rind
2 large egg whites
2 packets Equal®
2 cups frozen whipped topping,
    thawed slightly
Lemon rind (optional for garnish)

In small saucepan, stir lemon juice and gelatin; let stand 5 minutes. Heat mixture over medium heat, stirring, until gelatin is dissolved.

In large bowl, whisk egg yolks, 2 packets Equal®, and grated lemon rind until very light and lemon colored. Whisk in dissolved gelatin mixture.

In clean large bowl, with electric mixer at high speed, beat egg whites until frothy. Gradually beat in 2 packets Equal® and continue beating until shiny and stiff peaks form when beaters are lifted. Gently fold whites into lemon mixture. Fold in whipped topping until no white streaks remain. Cover and refrigerate at least 3 hours or overnight. To serve, spoon mousse into 8 glass dessert dishes. Garnish with lemon rind.

Makes 8 servings.
Calories per serving: 111.
Diabetic exchanges per serving: milk 0,
    vegetable 0, fruit 0, bread ½, meat 0, fat 1½.

Coffee Chiffon

2 envelopes (2 tablespoons) unfla-
    vored gelatin
½ cup water
2½ cups skim milk

3 egg yolks
1 tablespoon instant coffee crystals
½ teaspoon salt
4 packets Equal®
3 egg whites
1 teaspoon vanilla
¼ teaspoon cream of tartar
2 packets Equal®

Soften gelatin in ½ cup cold water. In medium saucepan, beat skim milk and egg yolks. Add instant coffee, salt, and softened gelatin. Cook and stir till mixture thickens and gelatin is dissolved. Remove from heat and stir in 4 packets of Equal®. Chill till partially set.

Beat egg whites, vanilla, cream of tartar, and 2 packets of Equal till soft peaks form. Fold in gelatin mixture. Spoon into 6-cup mold. Chill till firm.

Makes 10 servings.
Calories per serving: 55.
Diabetic exchanges per serving: milk 0,
vegetable 0, fruit 0, bread 0, meat 1, fat 0.

Tropical Parfaits

1 medium banana, sliced
Lemon juice
1 can (11 oz.) mandarin orange sections, drained
1 can (8 oz.) pineapple chunks (juice packed), drained
½ cup plain low-fat yogurt
2 packets Equal®
4 tablespoons unsweetened, grated coconut

Dip banana slices into lemon juice to prevent darkening. Mix fruit with Equal®. Layer yogurt and fruit mixture into 4 sherbet dishes. Sprinkle with coconut.

Makes 4 servings.
Calories per serving: 149.
Diabetic exchanges per serving: milk 0,
vegetable 0, fruit 2, bread 0, meat 0, fat ½

Chantilly Cream

2/3 cup heavy cream
1 teaspoon vanilla extract
1 teaspoon brandy
1 teaspoon Grand Marnier
2 tablespoons low-calorie sour cream
6 packets Equal®

Chill a medium-size bowl and beaters in the refrigerator until very cold. Combine cream, vanilla, brandy, and Grand Marnier in the bowl and beat with electric mixer on medium speed for 1 minute. Add sour cream and Equal®, and beat at medium speed just until soft peaks form, about 3 minutes. *Do not overbeat.* Makes about 2 cups.

Makes 4 (½-cup) servings.
Calories per serving: 165.
Diabetic exchanges per serving: milk 0,
    vegetable 0, fruit 0, bread 0, meat 0, fat 3.

You can vary the mousse flavor by using different flavors of yogurt

Piña Colada Mousse

1 container (8 oz.) frozen non-dairy
    topping, thawed
1 container (8 oz.) piña-colada-
    flavored low-fat yogurt
6 tablespoons unsweetened, grated
    coconut
2 packets Equal®

Spoon topping into a medium bowl. Gently fold in yogurt. Stir in Equal®. Divide mousse into 6 individual bowls. Top each with a tablespoon of coconut.

Makes 6 servings.
Calories per serving: 101.
Diabetic exchanges per serving: milk 0,
    vegetable 0, fruit 1, bread 0, meat 0, fat 1.

Rice Cream with Berries

> 1 cup rice
> 2 cups water
> ¼ cup low-calorie cream cheese
> ¼ cup low-calorie sour cream
> 1½ cups strawberries, raspberries,
>   blackberries, or blueberries
> 4 packets Equal®
> Milk crackers, such as croissant or
>   butter thins

Cook rice with water, following package directions, stirring constantly until tender. Remove from heat. Stir in cream cheese and sour cream. Fold in berries. Stir in Equal®. Spoon onto a platter and surround with crackers. Makes about 3 cups.

Makes 12 (¼-cup) servings.
Calories per serving: 50.
Diabetic exchanges per serving: milk 0,
    vegetable 0, fruit 0, bread ½, meat 0, fat 0.

Apple Mousse

> 1 teaspoon unflavored gelatin
> ½ of 6-oz. can (⅓ cup) frozen apple
>   juice concentrate
> ¼ teaspoon ground cinnamon
> 1 medium apple, cored, peeled, and
>   shredded
> ½ of 4-oz. container frozen whipped
>   dessert topping, thawed
> 1 packet Equal®

In a medium saucepan, soften gelatin in ⅔ cup of cold water for 5 minutes. Over low heat, stir mixture till gelatin is dissolved. Remove from heat. Stir in juice concentrate and cinnamon. Chill till partially set. Fold in apple, dessert topping, and Equal®. Spoon into 4 dessert glasses; chill till set.

Makes 4 servings.
Calories per serving: 35.
Diabetic exchanges per serving: milk 0,
    vegetable 0, fruit ½, bread 0, meat 0, fat 0.

Zesty Cream in Orange Shells

4 medium oranges
⅓ of 4-oz. container frozen whipped
    dessert topping, thawed
½ cup whipping cream
1 packet Equal®

Cut a very thin slice off bottom of each orange to make a flat base. Reserve these pieces to create orange zest for garnish. Cut off tops of oranges one-fourth of the way down; remove tops. Carefully scoop out pulp from tops and bottoms, reserving pulp, juice, and bottom shells. Set aside top shells of the oranges to use for garnish.

Place orange pulp and juice in blender container or food processor bowl. Cover; process till smooth. Fold in thawed whipped dessert topping. Pour mixture into a shallow pan; cover and freeze several hours or till orange mixture is firm.

Before serving, break up frozen orange cream; spoon into orange shell bottoms. Place shells in freezer. In small mixer bowl, beat whipping cream with Equal® until stiff peaks form. Remove oranges from freezer. Cover tops of oranges with whipped cream. Using a zester, scrape orange bottoms and sprinkle zest over cream. Take orange tops and place one top, slanted, over each orange.

Makes 4 servings.
Calories per serving: 91.
Diabetic exchanges per serving: milk 0,
    vegetable 0, fruit 1, bread 0, meat 0, fat ½.

Old-Fashioned Tapioca Pudding

3 tablespoons tapioca
⅛ teaspoon salt
1 egg yolk

2 cups skim milk
1 egg white
½ teaspoon vanilla extract
5 packets Equal®

Mix tapioca, salt, egg yolk, and milk in pan. Let stand 5 minutes. Beat egg white until soft peaks form. Set aside. Cook tapioca mixture over medium heat to a full boil, stirring constantly. Gradually add the beaten egg white, stirring quickly until well blended. Remove from heat, add vanilla and Equal®. Cool 20 minutes. Refrigerate until ready to serve. Garnish with fresh berries.

Makes 5 servings.
Calories per serving: 75.
Diabetic exchanges per serving: milk 0,
    vegetable 0, fruit 0, bread 1, meat 0, fat 0.

Pineapple-Cheese Mousse

3 tablespoons cornstarch
⅔ cup water
1 can (8 oz.) unsweetened crushed
    pineapple, undrained
1 teaspoon grated lemon peel
2 tablespoons lemon juice
2 egg yolks
3 oz. Neufchâtel cheese or low-calorie
    cream cheese
10 packets Equal®
2 egg whites

Combine cornstarch and water in medium saucepan. Stir until smooth; add pineapple and lemon peel. Cook over medium heat until mixture boils and thickens. Stir well. Remove from heat, stir in lemon juice and beaten egg yolks. Add cheese. Return to heat and continue cooking and stirring until mixture bubbles. Remove from heat, add Equal®, and beat with mixer to blend in cheese. Set aside to cool. Beat egg whites until soft peaks form. Fold into cooled pineapple mixture. Pour into champagne flutes and refrigerate until served.

Makes 6 servings.
Calories per serving: 108.
Diabetic exchanges per serving: milk 0,
    vegetable 0, fruit 1, bread 0, meat 0, fat 1.

Georgian Mousse

1 cup unsweetened canned peaches, drained
1 cup peach juice
2 teaspoons unflavored gelatin
6 packets Equal®
Diet whipped topping (optional)

Puree peaches in blender. In a small saucepan, soften gelatin in peach juice. Stir over low heat until gelatin dissolves completely. Chill until partially set. Fold in pureed peaches and Equal® and whip. Pour into glass dessert dishes and chill until firm. Garnish with whipped topping.

Makes 4 servings.
Calories per serving: 72.
Diabetic exchanges per serving: milk 0,
    vegetable 0, fruit 1, bread 0, meat 0, fat 0.

Snow Pudding with Custard Sauce

Pudding: **1 envelope unflavored gelatin**
            1¼ cups water
            ¼ cup lemon juice
            3 egg whites
            5 packets Equal®

Sauce: **1½ cups milk**
3 egg yolks
5 packets Equal®
½ teaspoon vanilla

To Make Pudding: Soften gelatin in ¼ cup cold water. Dissolve in 1 cup boiling water. Add lemon juice. Chill until mixture begins to set. Whip egg whites until stiff. Add the gelatin mixture and whip. Add Equal® and continue beating until mixture begins to stiffen. Chill thoroughly. Serve with Custard Sauce.

To Make Custard Sauce: In a heavy saucepan, beat together milk and egg yolks, using electric mixer or hand beater. Cook over medium heat, stirring constantly, until sauce thickens. Remove from heat and stir in Equal® and vanilla. Pour into bowl. Cover and refrigerate until chilled. Makes 1½ cups.

Makes 3 (½-cup) servings.
Calories per serving: 132.
Diabetic exchanges per serving: milk ½,
    vegetable 0, fruit 0, bread 0, meat 1, fat 0.

Bread Pudding with Raisins

1 envelope unflavored gelatin
2 cups milk
2 eggs slightly beaten
1 teaspoon vanilla
6 packets Equal®
2½ cups white bread cubes (about 4
    slices)
¼ cup raisins
¼ teaspoon nutmeg

Soften gelatin in ¼ cup milk. Scald remaining milk in top of double boiler. Add softened gelatin. Stir until gelatin dissolves completely. Pour hot milk slowly over eggs, stirring constantly. Return to double boiler, and cook over hot water until mixture coats a spoon. Remove from heat. Add vanilla and Equal®. Beat until frothy. Stir in bread cubes and raisins. Pour into 1½-quart mold that has been rinsed in cold water. Cover and refrigerate. At serving time, unmold and sprinkle with nutmeg. This dish can also be served with a fruit sauce (see page 33).

> *Makes 6 servings.*
> *Calories per serving: 130.*
> *Diabetic exchanges per serving: milk 0,*
>   *vegetable 0, fruit 1, bread 0, meat 1, fat 0.*

Frozen Desserts

When I think about frozen desserts, I remember most vividly the old-fashioned soda parlor, which seems to be making a comeback. Some of you may even remember when drugstores all had soda fountains, featuring sodas, shakes, sundaes, and, of course, banana splits. The soda parlor and the corner drug store were scenes of many childhood celebrations because ice cream seems to possess magical properties. Whether happy or sad, ice cream makes everything better.

Frozen desserts can be a dieter's paradise since many are made with fresh fruit and wholesome ingredients that are low in calories. Every cook's delight is an easy, do-ahead dessert. These selections of frozen mousses, pies, cakes, and ices are appropriate for every occasion. Imposing as they may appear, many of these desserts are not difficult to make, and many can be made hours or even days before you want to serve them.

Today, with our blenders, processors, and ready availability of ingredients, you don't have to budge from home to enjoy the most delicious frozen desserts.

Tips for Successful Frozen Desserts

- When selecting fruit, choose only the ripest to be sure the flavor and sugar content are fully developed. Fresh fruit is ideal but unsweetened frozen fruit can be substituted.
- To assure fine texture in your frozen desserts, stir the mixture ocassionally during the initial freezing process. The more you stir, the finer the texture.
- Taste the mixture after blending and adjust the sweetness according to taste.
- Ices and sorbets do not keep as well as ice cream and for best taste should be prepared no more than four days ahead.
- Pack ices firmly in container (to eliminate air pockets) when storing.
- Ices melt quickly so chill serving dishes and utensils.

How to Unmold Sherbet

1. Run a thin-bladed knife around the edge of mold or bowl. Invert mold onto a chilled serving plate.
2. Moisten a clean cloth under hot running water; wring out thoroughly; press cloth around side of the mold. Repeat several times until sherbet melts enough for mold to loosen; lift off mold. Return sherbet to freezer until serving time.

Serving Suggestions

- Set scoops of two or three sorbets of different colors on a plate, add some green leaves for color, and splash on fruit liqueur for pizazz.
- Spoon the ice or sherbet into hollowed-out melons or fruit cups, such as oranges or lemons. These containers can be frozen, and the sherbet won't melt as quickly.
- You can create a rainbow effect by layering different colors into an ice cream mold or metal bowl.
- For a more sophisticated dessert, layer freshly made ice or sherbet with mousse and ladyfingers to create a delicious Charlotte.

Strawberry Wine Ice

    2 cups whole fresh strawberries
    1 cup Chianti wine
    2 packets Equal®
    4 ice cubes
    4 whole strawberries (optional for
       garnish)

In blender container, process berries, wine, Equal®, and ice cubes until smooth. Pour mixture into a baking pan and freeze until slushy. Scrape mixture back into blender; process until smooth. Return to pan and freeze until firm. Soften about 5 minutes before serving.

This is a romantic, low-calorie dessert that should be garnished with a whole strawberry and served in a long-stemmed champagne flute.

> *Makes 4 servings.*
> *Calories per serving: 66.*
> *Diabetic exchanges per serving: milk 0, vegetable 0, fruit ½, bread 0, meat 0, fat ½.*

Lemon Sherbet ♥

    1 envelope (1 tablespoon) unflavored
       gelatin
    2 tablespoons cold water
    1½ cups skim milk
    ½ cup lemon juice
    Pinch salt
    10 packets Equal®
    ½ teaspoon lemon extract
    3 to 4 drops yellow food coloring
       (optional)
    1 egg white

Sprinkle unflavored gelatin over the cold water and wait for gelatin to soften. Heat milk in saucepan until it is steaming but not boiling. Remove milk from heat, add gelatin, and stir to dissolve. Add lemon juice, salt, Equal® lemon extract, and yellow food coloring. This mixture may curdle but do not be concerned.

Bring mixture to room temperature, pour into ice cube tray, and place in freezer for 1 hour. Do not let mixture freeze solid. Beat egg white until stiff peaks form. Transfer partially frozen mixture to a bowl and beat until fluffy but not melted. Fold in egg whites, pour into covered container, and freeze until firm.

Makes 4 (1-cup) servings.
Calories per serving: 60.
Diabetic exchanges per serving: milk ½,
  vegetable, fruit 0, bread 0, meat 0, fat 0.

Mint Sherbet ♥

1 envelope (1 tablespoon) unflavored
  gelatin
2 tablespoons cold water
1½ cups skim milk
10 packets Equal®
½ cup lemon juice
Pinch salt
¼ cup crème de menthe
1 egg white
Mint leaves, fresh (optional for
  garnish)

Sprinkle gelatin over cold water and wait for it to soften. Heat milk in saucepan until it is steaming but not boiling. Remove from heat, add gelatin and Equal®, and stir to dissolve. Add lemon juice, salt, and crème de menthe. Do not worry if mixture curdles.

Pour into ice cube tray and freeze for 1 hour. Do not let mixture freeze solid. Beat egg white until stiff peaks form. Transfer frozen mixture into a mixing bowl, and beat until fluffy but not melted. Fold in egg white, pour into covered container, and freeze.

Garnish with a fresh mint leaf, or try this in a Grass-hopper Shake (p. 26).

Makes 4 (1-cup) servings.
Calories per serving: 110.
Diabetic exchanges per serving: milk ½,
 vegetable 0, fruit 0, bread ½, meat 0, fat 0.

Berries in the Snow ♥

2 cans (16 oz.) pear halves in light
 syrup, undrained
¼ cup evaporated skim milk
1 cup sliced fresh strawberries
1 cup fresh blueberries
1 cup fresh raspberries
6 packets Equal®

Drain pears, reserving 1 cup liquid. Cut pears into cubes; place on an aluminum-foil-lined baking sheet; and freeze 2 hours or until firm. Place pears in container of an electric blender or food processor; cover and process 2 minutes. Gradually add remaining pear liquid and milk, processing until smooth.

Pour mixture into a 9-in. square pan. Freeze until firm, stirring every 30 minutes. To serve, spoon pear mixture into 8 individual serving dishes. Combine berries in a bowl and sprinkle with Equal®. Spoon over pear mixture.

Makes 8 servings.
Calories per serving: 90.
Diabetic exchanges per serving: milk 0,
 vegetable 0, fruit 1½, bread 0, meat 0, fat 0.

Watermelon Ice

4 cups cubed watermelon
⅓ cup cranberry juice cocktail
1 envelope unflavored gelatin
10 packets Equal®

Place watermelon cubes in blender container or food processor bowl. Cover and blend till smooth (should result in 3 cups of mixture). In a medium saucepan, soften gelatin in cranberry juice cocktail. Stir over low heat till gelatin is dissolved. Add gelatin to melon mixture; combine thoroughly. Pour mixture into an 8×8×2-in. baking pan. Cover; freeze for 2 hours or until firm.

Break up mixture; place in a chilled mixer bowl. Beat with electric mixer on high speed till mixture is fluffy. Return to pan. Cover; freeze at least 6 hours.

Makes 8 (½-cup) servings.
Calories per serving: 40.
Diabetic exchanges per serving: milk 0,
  vegetable 0, fruit ½, bread 0, meat 0, fat 0.

Coffee Ice ♥

2 tablespoons instant espresso
½ cup boiling water
1 cup cold water
6 packets Equal®
½ cup frozen whipped dessert topping, thawed
5 whole fresh strawberries (optional
  for garnish)

Dissolve coffee in boiling water. Stir in cold water. Stir in Equal®. Pour into a 9×5×3-in. loaf pan. Freeze about 2 hours or until firm.

Break frozen mixture into small chunks; place in chilled, small mixer bowl. Beat with electric mixer at low speed till fluffy. Freeze mixture till firm, about 2 hours. Scrape or scoop coffee ice into small goblets. Spoon whipped topping over each serving. Garnish with a strawberry.

Makes 5 (½-cup) servings.
Calories per serving: 40.
Diabetic exchanges per serving: milk 0,
    vegetable 0, fruit 0, bread 0, meat 0, fat 1.

Orange Sherbet ♥

3 cups skim milk
2 cups orange juice
2 tablespoons lemon juice
1 tablespoon grated orange rind
1 envelope unflavored gelatin
10 packets Equal®

In a large mixing bowl, combine all ingredients. Process in an ice cream maker according to manufacturer's directions. You can also pour into shallow pans, cover, and freeze until almost firm. Place in a large, chilled mixing bowl and beat with electric mixer until smooth. Return to pans. Cover with foil and freeze until firm. Makes about 1½ quarts.

Makes 12 (½-cup) servings.
Calories per serving: 46.
Diabetic exchanges per serving: milk 0,
    vegetable 0, fruit 0, bread ½, meat 0, fat 0.

Orange and Raspberry Ices ♥

Orange: 5 small juice oranges, scrubbed
        2 tablespoons frozen concentrated orange juice
        2 packets Equal®
        Orange slices (optional for garnish)

Raspberry: **3 cups fresh or frozen raspberries,
slightly thawed
4 packets Equal®
Raspberries (optional for garnish)**

To prepare orange ice, with serrated knife, cut rind and white pith from oranges. Working over large bowl, section oranges, letting sections and juice drop into bowl. Squeeze juice from membranes; discard membranes. Pour orange sections and juice into food processor or blender; add concentrated orange juice and ½ cup water; process until smooth.

Pour into an 8–9in. metal pan; discard seeds. Cover puree with foil, and freeze until frozen solid. One or 2 hours before serving dessert, remove orange ice from freezer to soften for a few minutes. Break into chunks and place in food processor or blender; process, using on-off switch, until snowy-textured. Scrape into freezer container; cover and freeze until ready to serve.

Repeat process for raspberry ice.

Let both ices soften a few minutes before scooping ⅛ of each (about ½ cup) into 8 dessert dishes. If desired, garnish each with an orange slice and 1 raspberry.

Makes 8 servings.
Calories per serving: 70.
Diabetic exchanges per serving: milk 0,
  vegetable 0, fruit 1, bread 0, meat 0, fat 0.

Blueberry Ice ♥

**½ envelope (1½ teaspoon) unflavored
  gelatin
1½ cups water, divided
1 package (10 oz.) unsweetened frozen blueberries, thawed
3 tablespoons lemon juice
6 packets Equal®**

Combine gelatin and 1 cup water in a medium saucepan. Place over medium heat, and stir until gelatin dissolves. Remove from heat, add remaining water, berries, lemon juice, and Equal®. Freeze until firm. Break into chunks; beat with mixer until smooth. Pour into freezer tray and freeze until firm. Let stand at room temperature 5–10 minutes before serving.

This ice can be made with raspberries, strawberries, or any combination of berries.

Makes 4 servings.
Calories per serving: 50.
Diabetic exchanges per serving: milk 0,
  vegetable 0, fruit 1, bread 0, meat 0, fat 0.

Frozen Cherry Yogurt ♥

24 cherries, fresh, pitted
2 cups plain low-fat yogurt
5 packets Equal®

Chop cherries (reserving 4 for garnish) in a blender or food processor. Add yogurt and Equal®, and blend on low setting until smooth. Freeze until firm.

Garnish with fresh cherries (optional).

Makes 4 (½-cup) servings.
Calories per serving: 90.
Diabetic exchanges per serving: milk 1,
  vegetable 0, fruit 0, bread 0, meat 0, fat 0.

Elegant Expectations

When it's lavish but easy to make, it's a great dessert. When it's delicious but low-calorie, it's a great dessert. When it's elegant but convenient, it's a great dessert. A dessert should be as delightful to look at as it is delicious to eat. This chapter will provide you with recipes that are lavish, low-calorie, delicious, and convenient as well as attractive to the eye.

Special occasions demand special desserts. It could be a birthday, promotion, birth of a baby, holiday, or the first day of summer! There's no better way to celebrate than with a spectacular dessert. They're all so good you won't know which to try first.

A treasure for coffee ice cream lovers!

Espresso Delight

> 1 egg white, chilled
> 1 tablespoon instant coffee crystals
> Dash of salt
> 8 packets Equal®
> ½ cup heavy cream
> 1 teaspoon vanilla extract
> ⅛ teaspoon almond extract
> ½ cup evaporated skim milk
> ¼ cup chopped walnuts

Beat egg white until it is frothy; add coffee and salt. Continue beating until soft peaks form. Add 3 packets Equal® and beat until white is stiff but not dry. Combine cream, remaining Equal®, and extracts. Beat until cream is stiff. Fold cream into beaten egg and coffee mixture. Beat evaporated milk until peaks form, and fold it into coffee mixture. Gently fold in nuts and pour into individual dessert dishes. Freeze until firm.

Garnish with a spoonful of whipped topping and a sprinkle of chopped nuts.

> *Makes 6 servings.*
> *Calories per serving: 125.*
> *Diabetic exchanges per serving: milk ½,*
> *vegetable 0, fruit 0, bread 0, meat 0, fat 2.*

Strawberry Ice ♥

> 4 cups fresh strawberries, hulled; or
>   unsweetened individually-frozen
>   strawberries, unthawed
> 6 packets Equal®
> 2 tablespoons fresh lemon juice
> 1 egg white
> 4 whole strawberries (garnish)

Halve 4 cups fresh strawberries and arrange in single layer on baking sheet. Freeze until firm, about 2 hours. Chop strawberries with Equal® in processor using on/off turns, then process continuously until slushy, about 5 minutes. With machine running, add lemon juice and egg white through feed tube and mix until light and thick, 2 to 3 minutes. Place bowl, covered, in freezer and freeze till firm, about 3 hours. Let soften a few minutes before serving. Scoop about ½ cup into glass dessert dish and top with a whole fresh strawberry.

> *Makes 4 servings.*
> *Calories per serving: 60.*
> *Diabetic exchanges per serving: milk 0,*
> *vegetable, fruit 1, bread 0, meat 0, fat 0.*

Mandarin Frozen Dessert

2 egg whites at room temperature
¼ cup frozen orange juice concentrate
2 packets Equal®
1⅓ cups graham cracker crumbs, or 16 (2-in.) squares, crushed
6 tablespoons diet margarine, softened
4 tablespoons finely-chopped walnuts
1 cup plain low-fat yogurt
½ cup mandarin orange sections (for garnish)

Beat egg whites with frozen orange juice and Equal® 7 minutes, using electric beater at medium speed. Meanwhile, combine graham cracker crumbs and margarine and stir in chopped nuts. Press crumb mixture on bottom and sides of 9-in.-square baking pan. Fold yogurt into the beaten egg-orange mixture. Pour into baking dish, and place in freezer at least 15 minutes.

Garnish with drained, unsweetened mandarin orange sections.

Makes 8 servings.
Calories per serving: 157.
Diabetic exchange per serving: milk 0, vegeta-
ble 0, fruit 0, bread 1, meat 0, fat 1½.

Coffee Meringues with Coffee Custard Filling

Shells: **4 egg whites**
          Pinch of salt
          4 teaspoons crème de cacao
          2 packets Equal®
          vegetable spray

Filling: **3 beaten egg yolks**
          ¼ cup nonfat dry milk
          2 teaspoons instant coffee crystals
          Dash salt
          2 packets Equal®
          1½ ounces diet dessert topping mix
          1 stiff-beaten egg white

To Make Shells: Place egg whites and salt in bowl. Beat together until frothy. Gradually add crème de cacao. Continue beating until whites are stiff, glossy, and stand in stiff peaks. Spray a 6-muffin tin with vegetable spray. Fill cups with meringue, hollowing out top of each with back of spoon. Bake at 250° for 1 hour. Remove from oven and dust with Equal®. Fill with Coffee Custard: refrigerate.

To Make Coffee Custard Filling: In small saucepan, combine egg yolks, milk, coffee, and salt. Cook over low heat, stirring constantly, till mixture coats a metal spoon. Remove from heat; stir in Equal®. Cool quickly by placing pan in a bowl of ice water; stir till mixture is cooled. Prepare topping mix according to package directions, except use skim milk or nonfat dry milk. Fold topping and egg white into cooled, cooked mixture. Chill. To serve, spoon into meringue shells.

Makes 6 servings.
Calories per serving: 63.
Diabetic exchanges per serving: milk 0,
  vegetable 0, fruit 0, bread 0, meat 1, fat 0.

Orange Parfait Cheesecake

Zwieback crust for 7-inch spring-form
  pan (page 77)
1 envelope unflavored gelatin
¼ cup water
2 beaten egg yolks
½ cup skim milk
⅓ cup ricotta cheese
⅓ cup orange juice
2 tablespoons orange liqueur
2 packets Equal®
1½ ounces diet dessert topping mix
½ cup skim milk
4 egg whites
2 packets Equal®

Prepare Zwieback Crust and set aside.

Soften gelatin in ¼ cup water. In a saucepan, combine egg yolks, skim milk, cheese, orange juice, and liqueur. Add softened gelatin. Cook and stir over medium heat about 20 minutes or until gelatin is dissolved and mixture coats a metal spoon; *do not boil.* Remove from heat: stir in 2 packets Equal®. Chill till partially set, stirring occasionally.

Prepare topping mix according to package directions; add the ½ cup skim milk; fold in gelatin mixture. In large bowl, beat egg whites with 2 packets Equal® till stiff peaks form. Fold in gelatin-topping mixture. Turn into crust-coated spring-form pan; cover and chill till firm. To serve, remove sides of pan, and sprinkle the reserved crumb mixture atop cheesecake.

Makes 10 servings.
Calories per serving: 180.
Diabetic exchanges per serving: milk 0,
  vegetable 0, fruit 0, bread 1½, meat 0, fat 1.

Fresh Fruit Trifle

1½ cups skim milk
½ cup 1% low-fat cottage cheese
2½ tablespoons cornstarch
2 tablespoons instant nonfat dry milk
2 teaspoons vanilla extract
Grated rind of 1 orange
3 packets Equal®
½ cup fruit-only strawberry jam
¼ cup orange-flavored liqueur
1 loaf (4 oz.) commercial angel food
  cake
2½ cups fresh strawberries, hulled
  and halved
2½ cups fresh blueberries
4 kiwi fruits, peeled and thinly sliced
4 medium oranges, peeled and
  sectioned
3 tablespoons coconut

Combine first 4 ingredients in container of an electric blender; cover and process until smooth. Pour mixture into top of double boiler; bring water to boil. Reduce heat to low; cook, stirring constantly, 10 minutes or until mixture thickens. Remove from heat; stir in vanilla, orange rind, and 3 packets of Equal®.

Combine strawberry spread and orange liqueur in a small saucepan; bring to a boil, stirring constantly. Remove mixture from heat and let it cool completely.

Trim crusts from cake, and cut into ½-in. slices. Line bottom of a 3-quart glass bowl with half the cake slices; brush with half of strawberry mixture. Arrange half the strawberries, blueberries, kiwi fruit, and oranges around the bottom edge of bowl on top of cake slices. Spoon half the cooled custard mixture over the fruit. Repeat this procedure with remaining ingredients. Cover and chill about 8 hours. Garnish with coconut.

Makes 12 (¾-cup) servings.
Calories per serving: 226.
Diabetic exchanges per serving: milk 0,
  vegetable 0, fruit 1, bread 2, meat 0, fat 0.

The color of this dessert is so beautiful that I like to serve it in clear dessert dishes.

Ruby Compote ♥

> 1 can (1 lb.) water-packed pitted tart
>   red cherries
> 1 tablespoon cornstarch
> Dash salt
> 1 tablespoon lemon juice
> 10 packets Equal®
> 4 drops red food coloring
> 1 pint fresh whole strawberries
> Sour cream (low calorie, as optional
>   garnish)

Drain cherries, reserving liquid. Add water to cherry juice to make 1½ cups. Blend together cornstarch, salt, and cherry juice mixture. Cook, stirring, till thickened and bubbly. Add lemon juice, food coloring, and Equal®. Stir in fruit and chill.

> *Makes 6 servings.*
> *Calories per serving: 54*
> *Diabetic exchanges per serving: milk 0,*
> *   vegetable 0, fruit 1, bread 0, meat 0, fat 0.*

Strawberry Cream Crepes

Prepare 1 batch of Dessert Crepes (see following recipe)

Filling: 3 ounces low-calorie cream cheese
           6 tablespoons 1% low-fat, dry-curd
             cottage cheese
           1 egg
           4 packets Equal®

Sauce: 2 cups fresh strawberries; or frozen
           unsweetened, thawed
         1 tablespoon lemon juice
         6 packets Equal®

To Make Filling: Place cream cheese, cottage cheese, egg, and Equal® in mixer. Blend until smooth; set aside.

To Make Sauce: Coarsely chop strawberries. Add lemon juice and Equal®. Toss lightly. When ready to serve, spoon 2 tablespoons filling into each crepe and roll. Arrange crepes, seam-side down, on plate. Serve immediately with fresh fruit sauce.

Makes 6 servings of 2 crepes each.
Calories per serving: 65.
Diabetic exchanges per serving: milk 0, vegetables
0, fruit ½, bread 0, meat ½, fat 0.

Dessert Crepes

2 eggs
¼ cup skim milk
2 tablespoons water
4 tablespoons all-purpose flour
⅛ teaspoon salt

Beat eggs, milk, and water. Add flour and salt; beat just till smooth. Spray a crepe pan with non-stick vegetable coating. Heat pan over medium heat. When pan is hot, spoon 2 tablespoons batter into pan and rotate pan to spread evenly. When edges of crepe are browned, turn crepe onto a plate. Makes 12 crepes.

Make desired filling and sauce (see preceding recipe).

Makes 6 servings of 2 crepes each.
Calories per serving: 46.
Diabetic exchanges per serving: milk ½,
vegetable, fruit 0, bread 0, meat 0, fat 0.

Strawberry Bavarian Crown with Ruby Glaze

Bavarian: 1 pkg. low-calorie strawberry gelatin
              1 cup hot water
              ½ cup ice water
              2 pkgs. (10 oz. ea.) frozen strawber-
                 ries; or 2½ cups sliced fresh
                 strawberries
              4 packets Equal®
              2 envelopes diet dessert topping mix
              1 baked angel food cake, 10-in. size

Glaze: 1 cup strawberry juice
              1 tablespoon cornstarch
              2 to 3 drops red food coloring
              1 teaspoon soft diet margarine

   To Make Bavarian: Dissolve gelatin in hot water, add
ice water, and chill until slightly congealed. Beat until
light and fluffy. Drain berries and reserve juice for
glaze. Stir in Equal®. Fold in strawberries and whipped
topping mix. Trim brown edges off angel food cake.
With fork, tear angel food cake into pieces. Alternate
cake pieces and gelatin mixture in a 10-in. angel food
cake pan. Chill until firm. Unmold on serving plate.
Drizzle with Ruby Glaze and chill.
   To Make Ruby Glaze: Blend cornstarch with a little
juice; gradually add to remainder of juice in a saucepan. Cook until clear, 3 to 5 minutes. Remove from
heat; add red coloring and margarine. Cool. Drizzle
over Bavarian Crown.

          Makes 12 servings.
          Calories per serving: 140.
          Diabetic exchanges per serving: milk 0,
             vegetable 0, fruit 1, bread 1, meat 0, fat 0.

Chocolate Mocha Cream Roll

Roll: ¾ cup sifted all-purpose flour
              1 teaspoon baking powder
              5 eggs, separated
              ⅛ teaspoon salt
              ½ cup brewed coffee
              ⅓ cup unsweetened cocoa
              5 packets Equal®

Filling: 1 envelope diet dessert whipped top-
                ping mix
              ½ cup skim milk
              2 teaspoons instant coffee crystals
              ½ teaspoon vanilla extract
              ½ teaspoon chocolate extract
              8 packets Equal®

To Make Roll: Spray bottom of a 15½ × 10½ × 1-in.
jelly-roll pan with vegetable spray. Line bottom with
waxed paper. Spray with vegetable spray. Preheat oven
to 400°. Sift together flour and baking powder onto a
piece of waxed paper. Reserve.

In a large bowl, at high speed, beat egg whites with
salt until until stiff peaks form. Beat egg yolks with
coffee and cocoa till well blended. Beat in reserved flour
mixture. Gently fold in beaten egg whites until no
white streaks remain. Turn batter into prepared jelly-
roll pan and bake 5 to 7 minutes. Test cake by tapping
center with your fingertip; cake should spring back
when done. Remove from oven and loosen cake around
edges with knife. Invert onto a clean towel, and peel
the paper from the cake carefully. Use a knife to help
peel off paper. Sprinkle cake with 5 packets of Equal®.
Place roll, seam side down, on rack. Cool. Meanwhile,
prepare filling.

To Make Filling: Combine whipped topping mix, skim
milk, instant coffee, vanilla, and chocolate extracts in a
deep, narrow-bottom bowl. Whip at high speed in electric mixer about 4 minutes or until topping is light and
fluffy. Add Equal® and stir to blend. Unroll cake, and

spread with filling. Re-roll without the towel and place seam side down on serving platter.

Makes 10 servings.
Calories per serving: 94.
Diabetic exchanges per serving: milk 0,
  vegetable 0, fruit 0, bread 1, meat 0, fat 0.

Coconut Custard-Filled Cake

Early in the day make the coconut custard filling so that it has time to set for about three hours before filling the cake.

Filling: **3 eggs**
   6 packets Equal®
   1 envelope unflavored gelatin
   2 tablespoons diet margarine
   ½ teaspoon vanilla
   1¼ cups skim milk
   ½ cup coconut toasted

Cake: **5 eggs separated**
   2 tablespoons water
   2 tablespoons lemon juice
   ½ teaspoon lemon peel
   ¾ cup all purpose flour
   1 teaspoon baking powder
   6 packets Equal®

To Make Filling: In blender, combine eggs, Equal®, gelatin, margarine, and vanilla. Blend on low speed about 30 seconds; scrape down sides. Heat milk to boiling. Cover blender, start motor, remove cover, and add hot milk slowly. Blend 10 seconds. Pour into a bowl, add coconut, and chill until set, about 3 hours.

To Make Cake: Beat egg yolks, water, and lemon juice until thick and lemon-colored. Gradually beat in lemon peel. Fold in flour and baking powder. Beat egg whites until stiff, but not dry, and peaks form. Fold into lemon mixture.

Spread batter on wax-paper-lined 11-×15-in. jelly-roll pan sprayed with non-stick vegetable spray. Bake in preheated 400° oven 10 to 12 mintues. Remove from pan immediately by inverting on a clean towel covered with aluminum foil. Remove wax paper and dust 6 packets of Equal® onto cake surface.

Remove filling from refrigerator and spoon onto cake, leaving a 2-in. border all around. Gently roll up cake jelly-roll style, using aluminum foil to assist in rolling. Secure ends of aluminum and twist. Place cake in refrigerator until you are ready to serve.

Makes one 10-inch roll, or 10 servings.
Calories per serving: 141.
Diabetic exchanges per serving: milk 1,
*   vegetable 0, fruit 0, bread 0, meat 0, fat 1.*

Della Robbia No-Bake Cheesecake

Graham Cracker Crust for 8-inch spring-form pan (page 79)

Filling: 1 tablespoon plus 1 teaspoon unflavored gelatin
1 tablespoon plus 1 teaspoon fresh lemon juice
1 tablespoon water
2 eggs separated, room temperature
½ cup skim milk
2 packets Equal®
Pinch of salt
2 cups 1% low-fat, large-curd cottage cheese
1¼ teaspoons vanilla
¾ teaspoon grated lemon peel
⅔ cup whipped diet dessert topping
6 packets Equal®
2 tablespoons apple jelly
2 teaspoons water
Assorted fresh fruit such as raspberries, sliced strawberries, seedless grapes, and orange segments.

Prepare Graham Cracker Crust and set aside.

Sprinkle gelatin over lemon juice and 1 tablespoon water in medium bowl. Whisk yolks to blend in small bowl. Bring milk and salt to a boil in heavy, small saucepan. Whisk milk into yolks, a little at a time. Return mixture to saucepan and stir over medium-low heat until custard thickens and coats the back of a metal spoon, about 6 or 7 minutes. Do not boil. Pour into a medium-size bowl. Stir in 2 packets of Equal®. Stir until gelatin dissolves.

Puree cottage cheese in processor or blender with half of the custard. Transfer to large bowl. Blend in remaining custard, vanilla, and lemon peel. Using electric mixer, beat whites in medium-size bowl until stiff peaks form. Gently fold into cheese mixture.

Prepare dessert topping mix and fold into cheese mixture. Sprinkle 6 packets of Equal® over mixture and mix well. Pour filling over crust. Cover and refrigerate overnight.

Stir apple jelly and 2 teaspoons water in heavy, small saucepan until slightly thickened.

Release sides of pan from cheesecake. Pat fruit dry and arrange in a decorative pattern over cake. Brush jelly glaze over fruit. Refrigerate.

Makes 10 servings.
Calories per serving: 160
Diabetic exchanges per serving: milk 0,
    vegetable 0, fruit 0, bread 1, meat 1, fat 0.

Rum Bavarian Pie

9-inch Graham Cracker Crust
(page 79)

Filling: **1 envelope unflavored gelatin**
¼ cup cold water
3 egg yolks
1½ cups skim milk
⅛ teaspoon salt

10 packets Equal®
½ teaspoon rum extract
3 egg whites
Chocolate curls or chopped nuts for
   garnish

Prepare crust and set aside.

Soften gelatin in water, about 5 minutes. Beat egg yolks and place in a small, heavy saucepan. Add milk and salt. Cook and stir over medium heat until mixture coats a metal spoon. Stir in Equal®, gelatin, and rum extract. Chill until mixture starts to thicken. Beat egg whites until stiff, and fold whites into filling. Pour into Graham Cracker Crust and chill several hours. Garnish with chocolate curls or some chopped nuts.

Makes one 8- or 9-inch pie.
Serves 8.
Calories per serving: 134.
Diabetic exchanges per serving: milk 0,
   vegetable 0, fruit 0, bread 1, meat 0, fat 1.

Banana Cream Pie

Zwieback Crust (page 77)

Filling: 3 egg yolks, beaten
          ¼ teaspoon salt
          2½ tablespoons cornstarch
          2 cups skim milk
          1 tablespoon diet margarine
          1 teaspoon vanilla
          5 packets Equal®
          2 ripe bananas, peeled and thinly
             sliced

Prepare Pie Crust and set aside.

Combine egg yolks, salt, and cornstarch. In a double boiler, scald milk. Pour milk slowly over egg mixture, stirring constantly. Return custard to top of double boiler and cook over hot water, stirring until it thickens. Remove from heat. Stir in margarine, vanilla, and Equal®. Place sliced bananas in bottom of Zwieback Crust. Pour custard on top. Chill before serving.

Makes one 8-inch pie.
Serves 8.
Calories per serving; 158.
Diabetic exchanges per serving: milk 0,
vegetable 0, fruit 1, bread 1, meat 0, fat 0.

Black Bottom Pie

Chocolate Crumb Crust (page 78)

Filling: 1½ envelopes unflavored gelatin (1½
            tablespoons)
            1½ cups skim milk, divided
            1 container (8-oz.) low-fat cottage
            cheese
            1 tablespoon vanilla extract
            10 packets Equal®, divided
            6 tablespoons cocoa powder
            3 egg whites
            Chocolate curls or sprinkles for
            garnish

Prepare Chocolate Crumb Crust and set aside.
Sprinkle gelatin over ¾ cup of the skim milk in a small saucepan. Soften 1 minute, then heat and stir until gelatin completely dissolves. Place cottage cheese in a blender or food processor; blend until completely smooth. Add gelatin mixture, remaining milk, and vanilla. Cover and blend till smooth, scraping down sides of blender occasionally.
Remove half of the blended mixture to a mixing bowl and set aside. To the half of the mixture remaining in blender, add 8 packets Equal® and the cocoa. Blend thoroughly, scraping down blender. Pour chocolate mixture into crust and chill until partially set, about 30 minutes.

Beat egg whites until stiff, but not dry. Gradually beat in remaining Equal®, then fold whites into the vanilla mixture in bowl. Spoon vanilla and egg white mixture over chocolate layer in crust. Chill several hours until set. Garnish with a few chocolate curls or chocolate sprinkles.

Makes one 9-inch pie.
Serves 8.
Calories per serving: 100.
Diabetic exchanges per serving: milk 1,
    vegetable 0, fruit 0, bread 0, meat 0, fat 0.

Strawberry Almond Pie

Custard
Filling:
- 2 cups skim milk
- 1 envelope (1 tablespoon) unflavored gelatin
- 2 egg yolks
- 2 tablespoons cornstarch
- 2 tablespoons cold water
- 1 teaspoon almond extract
- 2 packets Equal®

Strawberry
Filling:
- ½ cup fresh or frozen unsweetened strawberries
- 1 packet Equal®

Crust:
- 1 cup crushed corn flakes
- 2 tablespoons diet margarine, melted

If using frozen strawberries, thaw at room temperature, drain, and set aside. If fresh, wash, drain, and set aside.

To Make Custard Filling: Put the skim milk in top of double boiler and heat over moderate heat to just below boiling point, until bubbles begin to form around edge of pan. Sprinkle gelatin over hot milk, stirring well. Lightly beat egg yolks and add a small quantity of the hot milk. Add to pan. Dissolve cornstarch in the cold water and add to pan. Cook for about 10 minutes, stirring constantly, until mixture thickens. Remove from heat and add almond extract and Equal®. Set aside.

To Make Crust: Combine the crushed corn flakes and melted margarine, and press onto bottom of a 7-in. spring-form pan. Set aside.

To Make Strawberry Filling: Put strawberries into bowl of a food processor or blender and puree. Strain through a fine sieve to remove seeds; add Equal®.

Pour about half of the strawberry filling over crust, reserving the rest for garnish. Add custard filling, smoothing with a spatula. Drizzle the remaining strawberry filling over the custard in a circular motion to create a pattern. Refrigerate 6 hours before serving.

Serves 8.
Calories per serving: 126.
Diabetic exchanges per serving: milk 0,
    vegetable 0, fruit 1, bread 1, meat 0, fat 0.

Dessert Parties

How To Show Off Your Low-Calorie Creations

Anytime is a good time to discuss parties. Everyone loves a party, and if I'm going to be the hostess, I especially enjoy a dessert party. A dessert party allows you to be really creative, not only with food but also with the invitations, table setting, centerpiece, and decorations.

One of the benefits of a dessert party is that almost everything can be made in advance, leaving you to enjoy your guests. I bake cakes ahead, freezing them until the day of the party, and I make pies, cookies, and mousses the day before.

I suggest you prepare by making a list of the desserts you plan to serve. Be sure to include a variety such as pies, cakes, cookies, a mousse, and, of course, something chocolate. That way, you will have something for everyone. The success or failure of the party will depend on how much planning you put into it. Be sure to consider the size of your home. If space is at a premium, consider a buffet-style party, which works especially well for large gatherings.

Something else to consider is what beverages you will serve with each dessert. Punch, flavored coffees, and tea work well. In any case, you will need to plan ahead for your beverage selection, too.

The Perfect Setting

Before you plan the table setting, you might want to consider a theme for your party. One summer I held a Strawberry Festival Dessert Party. All the desserts included strawberries as part of the ingredients. To carry out the theme, the table was set with a white cloth, and I used ruby-colored glasses and white china. As the centerpiece, I filled silver berry baskets with fresh strawberries and silk flowers. Be sure to use cloth napkins; they are much more elegant than paper ones and hold up better, too.

The beverages served included strawberry tea, amaretto coffee, chocolate almond coffee, and herbal tea. I made the invitations myself, using red construction paper to fashion a large strawberry . . . what else?

Once when I was in school with very limited funds, I called my dessert party "The Fruits of Summer." At that time I did not own fine china or crystal, so I had to be creative when it came to the table setting. I planned to feature a menu of all fruit desserts, which I thought would be inexpensive.

The first thing I did was to make a list of all the desserts I wanted to serve, and beside each I listed the type of dish I would like to serve it in. It didn't take long to realize that I had a problem. Too many desserts and not enough dishes. That's when I got the idea to serve fruit desserts in real fruit "dishes."

A basket carved out of a watermelon featured Caribbean fruit salad. Melon halves served as dishes for cantaloupe mousse. A pineapple was used to display fresh Fruit Hawaiian. I used lemons, limes, and apples as dessert cups for lemon mousse, lime freeze, and apple mousse. I even had Cranberry Orange Dip served in hollowed-out oranges surrounded by fresh fruit.

I served the cakes and pies on clear glass plates, with paper doilies that I bought in the closeout section of a local department store. Instead of placemats, I used ti leaves that I got from the local florist.

To add some color, I bought napkins in a rainbow of fruit colors (about to be discontinued), which I picked up for a pittance. For the centerpiece, I chose a grove of tiny topiary trees, featuring small fruits: lady apples, strawberries, blueberries, kumquats, and grapes. I added some artificial leaves to make these more interesting. I strung paper lanterns around the table to complete the colorful decor.

I served fruit punch in a watermelon punch bowl and later served coffee. The chocolate dessert I served with coffee was chocolate-dipped strawberries. These were a big hit. A good time was had by all.

You can guess what a Chocolate Decadence Party might be like!

Serving Buffet Style

If a buffet is your choice, position the table so guests can move around it. If this is not possible, engineer it so guests move from left to right along the table and don't have to turn around. Set up a serving table off to the side so guests can pick up plates, napkins, and utensils before the food. Be sure to have all the right serving pieces and enough of them.

I like to set up a beverage station on a separate table. I usually put a sign in front of each drink so my guests know which flavors they're choosing, which coffee is decaffeinated, etc. If punch is served, use a recipe that won't overpower the dessert flavors. Be sure to indicate if the punch is spiked, and be sure to have plenty of ice.

I have one cardinal rule for a buffet party: serve desserts without gooey fillings or runny sauces.

If you are serving chilled desserts, place them over a bowl of ice to keep them fresh. The best way to do this is to take a square baking pan, fill it with water, and freeze it. Just before serving, bang the ice out onto the counter in one big piece. This can be put into a square crystal bowl, and it will provide a steady base for the individual dessert dishes. If you will be serving hot desserts, be sure to set out trivets.

I slice all the desserts into serving pieces before I place them—intact—on the buffet; then I place the first piece (the most difficult to remove) on a plate beside the rest of the dessert. This way, people are not shy about trying something since they don't have to fight to get at it.

I usually save a surprise for later in the party in case some guests come late or if it's someone's birthday or if I'm showcasing a recipe that I hope everyone will try.

If you give rise to your imagination, I am sure you can design a party that will combine delicious diet desserts, a creative table setting, and fond memories. You will also be able to say, "I did it all myself."

Recommended Brand Index

Cooking Oil: Mazola Corn Oil, manufactured by Best Foods, CPC International Inc., Englewood Cliffs, New Jersey.

Estee: The Estee Corp., Parsippany, New Jersey.

Extracts: Wagner's Extracts, distributed by John Wagner & Sons, Inc., Soyland, Pennsylvania.

Fruit-Only Jams: Sorrell Ridge, manufactured by Sorrel Ridge Farm, 100 Markley Street, Port Reading, New Jersey.

Gelatin: D-Zerta, distributed by General Foods Corp., 250 North Street, White Plains, New York.

Margarine: Weight Watchers brand, distributed by Nutrition Industries Corp., Cresskill, New Jersey.

Pancake Syrup: Featherweight brand, manufactured by Chicago Dietetic Supply Inc., La Grange, Illinois.

Sour Cream: Lean Cream, distributed by Land O' Lakes Inc., Arden Hills, Minnesota.

Vegetable Spray: Distributed by Boyle-Midway, Inc., 685 Third Avenue, New York, New York. Pam may be purchased in the cooking oil department of your supermarket

Whipped Topping: D-Zerta, distributed by General Foods Corp., 250 North Street, White Plains New York.

Index

Like Sugar-Free Cooking?
Then you'll love the <u>original</u>
Free and EQUAL.
Cookbook.

If you enjoyed the delicious desserts and treats in this book, you'll be pleased to know that you can extend the benefits of sugar-free cooking to your entire menu! The original Free and Equal® Cookbook contains more than 150 mouth-watering, low-calorie recipes for appetizers, soups, salads, sauces, entrees, desserts, drinks—even snacks and breakfast treats. Each dish substitutes Equal®, the good-tasting, saccharin- and sodium-free sweetener for sugar. Calorie counts and diabetic exchanges are given for each easy-to-make recipe. So if you love tasty food but can do without the empty calories of sugar, order Carole Kruppa's original Free and Equal® Cookbook today!

Notes & Recipes

Notes & Recipes